ALASKAN LOVE STORIES: A Researcher's Life

Dena Rose Matkin

ALASKAN LOVE STORIES: A Researcher's Life
© 2013 Dena Rose Matkin

ISBN 978-1-890692-24-7

Book editing, design and layout by Jan O'Meara

Front cover photo Transient killer whale female and calf by Dena Matkin.
Photo p. 5 by Bruce Mettler.
Photo p. 150 Black-legged kittiwake adult and juvenile by Dena Matkin.
Drawings pp. 148-153 by Dena Matkin:
    Harbor porpoise
    Spyhopping orcas
    Puffins
    Harbor seals
    Steller sea lions.
Photo p. 266 by Kate Boesser.
Back cover photos:
    Killer whale breaching by Debbie Broeckling.
    Dena Matkin by Eve Matkin.
    Eve Matkin and Orca pup by Dena Matkin.

Any errors of fact or omissions are purely accidental and unintentional. The author apologizes in advance for any misspellings of names herein.

All rights reserved. No part of this book may be reproduced or transmitted in any form or by any means, electronic or mechanical, including photocopying, recording, or by any information storage and retrieval system, without written permission of the author. Book reviewers have permission to reprint excerpts and photos within the body of their review and to publish the same as a review.

Wizard Works
Homer, Alaska

TABLE OF CONTENTS

Dedication 5
Acknowledgements 7
Prologue 9
Introduction 13

PART ONE: LETTERS FROM MY LIFE 15
Chapter 1:   Finding ourselves and going to Alaska 17
Chapter 2:   Happy Homer homesteaders 31
Chapter 3:   Falling in love with Prince William Sound 69
Chapter 4:   Cordova and Cape Espenberg letters 79
Chapter 5:   Glacier Bay, Gustavus and Eve wisdom 119
Chapter 6:   Mama story 141

PART TWO: PHOTOS, DRAWINGS AND STORIES 145
Chapter 7:   Messages from New Zealand 155
Chapter 8:   Eve wisdom from Eugene, Oregon 185
Chapter 9:   Why me? 189
Chapter 10: Memoriam 197
Chapter 11: Dogs, bears and moose musings 205
Chapter 12: Killer whale love stories 211
Epilogue 237

Southeastern Alaska killer whale names 253
Bibliography / Alaskan killer whale references 261

For my sister Barbara who taught me so many things, especially about love.

The day after your birthday in mid-July the hermit thrush stops singing my favorite song. I miss that soft yodeling flute's sweet echoes as much as I miss you.

ACKNOWLEDGEMENTS

I would like to thank Eve Matkin, Craig Matkin, the late Doris Haskell, Kirk Haskell, the late Dorothy Matkin, Sean Neilson and Greg Streveler for their written contributions.

For giving assistance, knowledge or inspiration thanks to my father the late Del Haskell for saving my letters, and in alphabetical order: Paul Atkinson, Scott Baker, Ken Balcomb, Lance Barrett-Lennard, the late Michael Bigg, Marylou Blakeslee, Kate Boesser, Nate Borson, Craig Conger, Lynne Cox, Marilyn Dahlheim, Alisha Decker, Volker Deecke, Nat Drumheller, Bill Eichenlaub, Jennie Engebretsen, Graeme Ellis, John Ford, Bertha Franulovich, Christine Gabriele, Laurel George, John Granan, Ken Grant, Mike Greenfelder, Christophe Guinet, Alice Haldane, Lee and Linda Haskell, Wilf Hatch, Carol Haykus, Margaret Hazen, Kim and Melanie Heacox, Kathy Heise, Justin Hofman, Betty Hunter, John Hyde, the late Pete Islieb, the late Mark Jacobs, Jr., Lauri Jemison, Eivin Kilcher, Pat Leary, John Lemberg, Linda Lieberman, Jodi Miller, Barbara Morford, Alexandra Morton, Emily Mount, Carlos Navarro, Janet Neilson, Mike Nigro, the late Ken Norris, Jan O'Meara, Kimber Owen, Pete and Gretchen Pederson, Anjanette Perry, Karen Platt, Jan Roderick, Peter Rumm, Eva Saulitis, Johanna Schot, Bill Shadley, Fred Sharpe, Justin Smith, Andy Spear, John and Jan Straley, Jack Swenson, Mike and Karen Taylor, Jared Towers, Andrew Trites, Phoebe Vanselow, Ingrid Visser, Olga von Ziegesar, Paul Wade, Harald Yurk, and the Glacier Bay National Park and Preserve whale sighting network.

For continued support in the form of Scientific Research Permits thanks to the National Marine Fisheries Service/National Oceanic and Atmospheric Administration and Glacier Bay National Park and Preserve. For support in the form of funding for my killer whale research, thanks to the North Gulf Oceanic Society, University of Alaska, University of British Columbia Marine Mammal Research Unit, National Park Service, National Marine Mammal Laboratory/Seattle, Fisheries and Oceans' Pacific Biological Station/British Columbia, Canada, and the United States Marine Mammal Commission.

PROLOGUE

Early spring, 2005 — Gustavus, Alaska

On my birthday in October two years ago my only sister, Barbara, was diagnosed with a brain tumor. Suddenly it was time to tear myself away from the joys of a southeastern Alaska autumn (joys if you like serious weather pounding down on breathtaking landscapes) and fly south to visit family in central California.

In between walks and talks with my recovering older sister, and during the time staying at my parents' nearby home, my mother showed me some boxes of photos and letters my father had saved. Things he had treasured and kept on or in his desk were now put away and temporarily forgotten since his death in 1998.

Much to my amazement, I realized he really had saved just about every letter I ever wrote home. I vaguely remembered him saying something to that effect once, indicating my story might be worth telling in book form. My flippant perspective at that point in time was that my life seemed more like a silly melodrama than anything else. I continued on with the business of life, which in my case meant staunchly maintaining my well-earned title of "Gypsy of the Family."

As I began reading those past letters to my parents and three siblings, two things became immediately clear: One, I had been a very conscientious daughter (and sister) about communicating my dreams and many of my various adventures, especially of going to live in Alaska. Of course, my mother's most enduring memory of me seems to be as a rebellious fifteen year old, no matter what I've done to redeem myself since.

And, two, as I gasped at the long-forgotten photos that fell out of those old letters, I realized that by sharing with my family, my earliest years in Alaska thirty years previous had been preserved. A fire had consumed the log cabin containing our worldly possessions as my new husband and I attended classes at the University of Alaska in Fairbanks in the winter of 1977. What we had before that was gone, except our skis.

Upon returning to my home of twenty-five years near Glacier Bay, Alaska, with my pile of letters and renewed memories, I began to look for more letters, cards, essays and poems that had been written through the years. As I began putting it all in chronological order, something else emerged: I was most inspired to write when feeling happy and grounded in a beautiful place. Traumas such as the fire were not mentioned in any of my letters. Things like divorce, a life-threatening disease or politics were minimized. An essay my mother wrote as a presentation to her close friends about my life in Alaska fills in some of those gaps from her perspective.

There are dark times of loss, uncertainty or frustration in everyone's life story, but that is not what this book is about. First written as therapeutic journals, then later used as fire starter in the heat stove, my journals that chronicle some of the hardest times thus served several practical purposes. The irrepressible poetry of love, forgiveness and the healing powers of nature that came, sometimes, a decade later became more worth sharing. The unbridled delight of traveling with my daughter Eve (the new "Gypsy of the Family") inspired e-mails to my younger brother, Kirk, in Oregon from Eve and me in New Zealand the winter after she graduated from high school.

It was the immediacy of letters and essays written at the time that captured my imagination for the structure of a book: Let the original writing tell a story about my falling in love with a man, with Alaska, with my daughter and with the local killer whale population. I often wonder how many times I have been in a place that would later defy description, but because I was so cold or scared out of my wits (or both) I was unable to hold pen, pencil or camera to document it all. What I have brought away from those times was the thrill of being alive after all, and the images and feelings I tried to brand into my brain and my heart at the time.

After I was engulfed in motherhood in 1983 and finally had a telephone, writing letters home to my parents became less of a priority. And later, studying the killer whales necessitated more writing in the form of scientific papers. Fortunately, my daughter Eve had a writing style that began flowing at an early age, offering the wisdom of a child's perspective on being raised in the Alaskan bush.

So many of my most memorable times out on the water are relegated to a few cursory lines in my yellow field notebook. There is nothing about the life-changing power and beauty of the forces of full moon, ebbing tides and westerly winds that conspired to produce breaking swells large enough to nearly engulf my 20-foot research vessel, the *Kingfisher* (my mom's favorite bird). But, no worries, though my 80-something-year-old mother likely remembers that time as her most white-knuckled Alaskan visit with me, we got home just fine with the data that made it all worthwhile.

It had been my mother's secret wish, since about age eighteen, to move to Homer, Alaska, and grow turnips, after she first started reading about the place. Her life took her in other directions, not the least of which was having me, but the seed of that dream reached fruition when I answered the call of the North a generation later.

There are no copious notes in my field notebook regarding the unforgettable time my black Labrador retriever named Orca (white spot on his chest) dove off the bow into the path of an oncoming group of transient (mammal-eating) killer whales. There is a brief line about the whales submerging and going on their way, but nothing about my hysterical shrieking as I backed the boat toward my beloved thrashing canine companion and tearfully scolded the dripping 100 pound beast as I hauled him back on board.

The killer-whale-encounter stories are based on more than twenty-five years of field notes expanded onto the daily encounter forms I fill out at the end of a day's work out on the water. Those stories represent the times I thought the whales had taught me something I may actually have understood. With killer whales, the day can easily end with more questions than answers. However, when the photographs and prey remains are later identified, the mysteries of these groups' lives sometimes begin to unravel.

The killer whale names at the end of the book are names I (and others) have given to some of the killer whales that inhabit southern Alaska. They mostly represent local place names, people, other animals, physical or behavioral characteristics. Tlingit language names honor the local native population. Other languages are also represented. Naming whales is not to imply that they mirror us, but many people may identify with them as complex fellow mammals, and human words are a tool we have to describe them. Besides helping me keep track of who's who, naming each killer whale reinforces the fact that each is an individual with potentially life-long family bonds that interacts intensively with all the other life forms in its changing ocean world.

INTRODUCTION

In the fall of 1970 I turned twenty-one, and took a temporary leave of absence from college. My parents (Del and Doris Haskell) took what must have been temporary leave of their sanity, and gave me the use of the old 1955 Chevy Carryall that had been the family truck when we were all learning to drive. My older brother Lee now maintains it in perfect condition in spite of my dedicated efforts to age it.

My mission that fall was to drive alone from California to the East Coast of the United States and back in search of beautiful wild places, historical sites and unknown adventures. One letter from that trip is where my stories begin. It crystallizes my frame of mind at the time in a way I could never do just trying to remember it all.

But the spark to see new things began at a much earlier age, when I traveled by bus from what was then home in Independence in eastern California to visit my grandmother Grace (mother's mother) in Rosemead in southern California. My happy enthusiasm at being "out in the world" at age eight was in a letter dated June 14, 1958:

Dear Family,
Thursday I had the best sleep I ever had in a long time. Friday we went to Olivera Street. I had a tuna sandwich for lunch and after that I had a candy apple. But I really wanted cotton candy. And I have a surprise that Grandma bought for me. You guys will adore it. And Grandma bought me a jump rope at toy town. And guess how many hours it took me to eat my candy apple? Then Knott's Berry Farm and ghost town came into our minds. We went to Holy places. And we went on the train, and the bandit came on too and when they shot their guns they almost made my head pop off. And the part I liked best was the haunted shack. We, that is Grandma and I, with some other people went together and a chair just like a magnet to the wall stood there and you could not believe in front of your eyes a ball roll up hill. And we saw an old school house.
That is the end of my story. Mama when are you coming down to get me?
From Dena Rose

After I graduated from the University of California at Santa Cruz with a Bachelor's degree in Science, my sole mission in life was to go to Alaska. It was not hard to convince my college sweetheart that this was a good idea. With backpacks on our backs, we headed North in June 1974. My "itchy feet" have taken me many amazing places in the world: Canada, Hawaii, Mexico, New Zealand, Australia, Fiji, Galapagos, Peru, Belize, Guatemala, Bahamas, France and Scotland.

But no place, however beautiful, ever made me feel the way I felt upon first arriving in Alaska: "Yes, I am home!" I could spend the rest of my life happily exploring the parts of Alaska I have never seen. Well, in between exploring the infinite behaviors of the killer whales that come into my life.

My stories end when my daughter Eve is almost twenty-nine. She graduated from the University of Oregon with a Bachelor's degree in Psychology to ultimately practice art and wilderness therapy with children. How itchy are her feet? Very. Her dreams may take her to India, Tibet, Central and South America. Her insight may heal broken lives. Her sweetness may inspire more love stories. More than anything, she is a child of Alaska, grounded in love for a place whose beauty helped create her nurturing spirit.

PART ONE: LETTERS FROM MY LIFE

CHAPTER 1: FINDING OURSELVES AND GOING TO ALASKA

September, 1970
Upstate New York

Hi Folks,

 Can you come down off the walls for a minute to read a letter? Here I am being treated like a queen. Joanna and I have talked non-stop for about five days now. Old friends are the most valuable things one can find when so far from home. Both of us are really feeling that now... her missing people in Modesto terribly, and my feeling rather homeless.

 My lives are all passing before me... converging, dispersing. Making me laugh and cry. And wonder and dream of what next? I'm still looking for him that is kind and gentle and handsome and intelligent and capable and curious and mustached and happy and thoughtful and humble and simple and strong and quiet and energetic and dependable, with a passionate love of nature and her glories, and with a heart as big as all the universe, and who loves me more than anything else. That's all.

 But for now, Sol will do. He almost lives up to it all. He's the best buddy I could ever hope for. I got him his first distemper shot the other day. One more to go. Everyone loves him. He's almost housebroken, and just the perfect little traveler. He's always making me laugh... a real nut.

 I'll be going up to Vermont and New Hampshire later on. The fall color should be getting down to the southern parts of them in a week or so.

 Lotsa driving tomorrow, and it's bedtime... so g'nite and sweet dreams for tomorrow.

 Love, Dena

February 14, 1973
Yosemite National Park,
California

To Craig:

Huge soaring birds and fields of mustard,
Brand new snow and still snowing…
what a delight.
I sure hope you are loving it all…
not much doubt that you are.

Running into so many old friends,
makes one stop and think of new friends…
and smile.
Who are you? Hello.

XOXO, Dena

March, 1973
Santa Cruz, California

Dear Mama and Daddy,

    I got your letter last week, and all in it made me smile… the article, the news of what you're doing. Yes, Mama, you can get organic oranges at the co-op here. I'll bring some home soon.
    I filled my gas tank with the money you sent… just in time! I will not hitchhike alone anymore, if at all, don't worry. Thank you so much for your concern… I love you.
    Mostly I just have to tell you how happy I am right now. I feel like I've found something I've never really known before. Maybe hard for you to take seriously, but I like Craig so much, I'm just filled to the brim. And what's so far out is that he feels exactly the same… neither of us can believe that we could be so lucky.
    We met in Geology lab here at UCSC, and we never seem to run out of things to talk about that interest us both. Since four days we spent together in Mammoth, skiing, we have been together almost constantly, and can't understand why we're not tired of each other. It has grown so naturally, with no pushing or trying or pressure from either of us. It seems to be a force or an entity completely independent of us, yet within us, too.
    I think I am beginning to understand why people get married. They feel so much love for each other, it would take at least a lifetime to express it all. Both of us really want it to last, and try not to do anything that might blow it.
    Last weekend we went cross-country skiing in Sequoia with some people in a mountaineering class through school. Fun, but one of the most strenuous trips I've been on yet. We camped in tents in the snow. Sunday was sunny and beautiful, and until afternoon the snow was perfect to ski on.
    I had a dream about Barb last night. She was singing "If I Had a Hammer" on her guitar and dancing around and being really crazy. It was fun seeing her that way. Maybe you could show Barb this letter and it would inspire her to write to her dear little sister.
    Got my paper on the northern lights back, and the professor liked it… he said it was a "very good paper, showing much work."

I'll bring it home for you to read soon.

If possible, try not to worry about me, although I can understand why you would, with insanity abounding in this world. I am well protected by a 6' 1", 165-pound blond-haired, blue-eyed angel. I'm also eating better than ever, and always have enough.

Yea, Kirk… I sure hope I can see you motorcycle race sometime soon. You're so far out… I'm glad you're my brother.

Love to everyone, Dena

August, 1973
Sunshine Mesa, Colorado

Dear Kirk,

A rainy day. Today we have spent most of the day in the tent, goofing around, playing cards and reading. Sounds real exciting, huh? It's been raining for two days now. It stopped just long enough to go out and eat breakfast, then back to the tent. Yesterday evening when it stopped for a while, we took a walk... there was snow on the tops of all the peaks, even some on Sunshine Mountain!

Everyone is saying it's going to be an early winter, and I believe it. Some of the aspen are beginning to turn. Wow... I wish we could be here long enough to see a Colorado fall. Probably catch some of it, at any rate, before we have to leave so Craig can make it back to school in Santa Cruz.

We recently got back from hiking through the Never Summer range... really incredible mountains. Quite a bit of snow and tons of wildflowers. We (including Sol) climbed the highest peak in the area... Mt. Richtoffen (12,940 ft.). The names of the other peaks are really neat... Mts. Cirrus, Cumulus, Nimbus, Stratus. We are leaving for the Gores to hike soon, then will be back here at our campsite on Sunshine Mesa to spend the rest of our time before returning to California.

I wish you could see it here. Finding our summer place was worth waiting for, after much searching. We are about 10 miles from the nearest town, most of that on dirt roads and the last two miles on foot, which involves a river crossing. (Putting everything on your head, and wading barefoot through the rushing water about knee deep). Only trouble with it... gads, the mosquitoes! We are both just a mass of bumps... itch, itch! But I think we are even getting used to that.

We have been bathing in the ice-cold streams from the snow melt...brrr! Really feels good after it's over, though — Even here at 9,000 ft. Craig caught his first fish of the year a couple weeks ago, and, boy, was he happy. A brown trout, I think. The beaver ponds nearby are excellent for fishing, so I guess I'll have to go try my hand at it soon. We have been eating well, and, of course, my appetite has about quadrupled since we got here.

    We aren't really looking forward to leaving Colorado. It has been a good summer for us, compared to the hardships others have been faced with. We've mostly been able to do what we like best: hiking, climbing, naming the flowers and birds, picking all kinds of berries and loving each other. Being outdoors! Seems like one rarely gets all the things one loves all in one place. We are very thankful for this time we have been given. Time that gives faith in goodness, cleanness and the wholeness of things.

    See you in September. You'll probably be in school when I get back, but I'll be around for a little while before I go up to Yosemite to work at the ski area for the winter. Have you read my thesis yet?... ha! Hang tight, hang loose, whatever.

    Love, sister Dena

November, 1973
Yosemite, California

Dear Mama,

I'm really liking my job here… whew! what a load off! I'm so happy I'm working, I don't even mind not being able to go to the Channel Islands.

Hope your Thanksgiving was nice. Craig and I had a quiet little banquet that night. Candles, wine, etc. Last night we went ice skating. What a gas! I do love it. He's been skiing every day and left this morning. Not many clear days since you left. It's snowing in the Valley right now.

But I sure miss Craig… each time I see him it's better and each time I leave him it's harder. I've never felt this way about anyone. Our relationship seems so complete (as he put it). It will be wonderful to be with him all the time again.

I just found out today all employees who work at Badger Pass get a free season ticket on the ski lifts, so I may be doing a little more downhill skiing this winter.

I've been thinking about starting a recycling project up here.

Tomorrow I have off and I am going cross-country skiing for the first time this year… yea! Will be in touch through letters.

Love, Dena

July, 1974
Santa Ana, California

Dear Doris and Del (Haskell),

It was so thoughtful of you to write and keep us posted as to Dena and Craig's whereabouts. I am so glad they made connections. We, too, received a letter written July 4, 1974. They were on the ferry leaving Juneau on their way to Haines, then to begin the trip into the interior and then down the Kenai Peninsula to Homer. They are both very considerate to write. Craig is very enthusiastic about the country already.

I do appreciate your sharing your thoughts and feelings about these two. Dena is a lovely, warm, loving, considerate person with great empathy for others and we like her very much. I can certainly understand your feelings about their relationship. We feel very much the same but, of course, with Craig being the male there is a little difference in concern. I feel so strongly as you indicated, too, that there should be stability of purpose in life. One should be fulfilled, of course, but it should be fulfillment of one's potential as well as personal.

Craig has always met the obligations of his existence, has been a top honor student throughout his schooling, and been extremely sensitive and responsible in all other areas, working while in school, etc. Now it would seem he should develop to his fullest and become trained in his field so that he can really contribute to his field and not just be one who has a smattering of knowledge and content with aimless hit or miss productivity.

This is his first break in schooling, and a deserved one. Our concern is that he not consider this a way of life. I agree with you that a profession of some kind for both woman and man is fulfilling and beneficial to society and hopefully they both will come to that way of thinking. I do think their relationship is a deep one and would seem to be one which will lead to permanency.

But, of course, we both realize that there is more than one way, and that these two individuals have the right to find it for themselves. We want the most and finest for them but at this stage

November, 1973
Yosemite, California

Dear Mama,

I'm really liking my job here… whew! what a load off! I'm so happy I'm working, I don't even mind not being able to go to the Channel Islands.

Hope your Thanksgiving was nice. Craig and I had a quiet little banquet that night. Candles, wine, etc. Last night we went ice skating. What a gas! I do love it. He's been skiing every day and left this morning. Not many clear days since you left. It's snowing in the Valley right now.

But I sure miss Craig… each time I see him it's better and each time I leave him it's harder. I've never felt this way about anyone. Our relationship seems so complete (as he put it). It will be wonderful to be with him all the time again.

I just found out today all employees who work at Badger Pass get a free season ticket on the ski lifts, so I may be doing a little more downhill skiing this winter.

I've been thinking about starting a recycling project up here.

Tomorrow I have off and I am going cross-country skiing for the first time this year… yea! Will be in touch through letters.

Love, Dena

January, 1974
Yosemite, California

Hello Folks,

    Happy Anniversary! To commemorate your anniversary this year, I am sending the last of the amount I owe you. I will even try to pay for some phone calls in the future.

    This weekend is Craig's and my anniversary, too. A whole wonderful year exactly. He just wrote and said he's coming up Thursday or Friday… I'm so glad.

    He is going to be the Teaching Assistant for the Natural History class this spring. Ken Norris really wanted him to. We've both sent our applications in to McKinley National Park. Now just hoping. The chances are so slim.

    I'm getting into downhill skiing lately…wow, such a gas! The other day was perfect: brand new snow and clear sunny skies. I'm still at heart a cross-country skier, but this is neat while it's available.

    Doing a lot of reading on Alaska, too. Craig's parents gave me a beautiful book on Alaskan wildlife for Christmas. I'm reading that and hungry for more.

    Just started a ceramics class being given up here tonight. Really good to get back into that.

    See you sometime next month. Let me know when.

    Love, Dena

April, 1974
Yosemite, California

Hello All Haskells,

Happy Birthday, Lee! Sorry for the neglect at letter writing… finally getting around to it after a couple of weeks of Craig-concentration. My favorite way of spending time. I got five days off in a row just as he got here, so we went to the area around Kirkwood on highway 88. One day downhill skiing which was sunny and not too many people at all; and the rest of the days cross-country skiing and snow camping out from Kit Carson Pass.

Great weather the whole time. Spent the time skiing through meadows, climbing up high ridges and skiing down them. Sol came along, too, which was great being with him for so long. The last day, Craig broke the tip off his brand new skis (bummer), so now he has to buy new ones. All my cross-country ski equipment is getting pretty funky by now, so I will have to get the whole package. I will leave them with you for the summer, then you can send them up to me in Alaska next winter.

Our move to Alaska is only about two months away now, and we are preparing the best we can: making ferry reservations, reading lots of books, ordering special rain boots and pants, but mostly trying to save $$$! I have the job at the Mountain Shop this spring, and will start there in a couple weeks or so.

Craig had to leave his bike until I can get it down to him, so now I ride around the loop in the Valley each evening after work. It looks like Mother Nature is making up for a fairly light winter by giving us a stormy spring. For the last couple weeks we've had storm after storm, with a rare day of sun now and then.

It is definitely spring here, though, at the lower elevations. On a walk up off one of the trails last week, Craig and I found gardens of mosses and monkey flowers.

By the way, he may be graduating with honors (ta da!), so we might stay around for that in June. If so, you're invited so that you can meet the Matkins… maybe we'll do a dinner thing or something.

See you soon, probably.
Love, Dena

July, 1974
Santa Ana, California

Dear Doris and Del (Haskell),

It was so thoughtful of you to write and keep us posted as to Dena and Craig's whereabouts. I am so glad they made connections. We, too, received a letter written July 4, 1974. They were on the ferry leaving Juneau on their way to Haines, then to begin the trip into the interior and then down the Kenai Peninsula to Homer. They are both very considerate to write. Craig is very enthusiastic about the country already.

I do appreciate your sharing your thoughts and feelings about these two. Dena is a lovely, warm, loving, considerate person with great empathy for others and we like her very much. I can certainly understand your feelings about their relationship. We feel very much the same but, of course, with Craig being the male there is a little difference in concern. I feel so strongly as you indicated, too, that there should be stability of purpose in life. One should be fulfilled, of course, but it should be fulfillment of one's potential as well as personal.

Craig has always met the obligations of his existence, has been a top honor student throughout his schooling, and been extremely sensitive and responsible in all other areas, working while in school, etc. Now it would seem he should develop to his fullest and become trained in his field so that he can really contribute to his field and not just be one who has a smattering of knowledge and content with aimless hit or miss productivity.

This is his first break in schooling, and a deserved one. Our concern is that he not consider this a way of life. I agree with you that a profession of some kind for both woman and man is fulfilling and beneficial to society and hopefully they both will come to that way of thinking. I do think their relationship is a deep one and would seem to be one which will lead to permanency.

But, of course, we both realize that there is more than one way, and that these two individuals have the right to find it for themselves. We want the most and finest for them but at this stage it seems we must be supportive bystanders. I do so appreciate your writing and look for more in the future.

Fondly, Dorothy Matkin (Craig's mom)

July, 1974
Southeastern Alaska

Dear People,

    Hello down there. Wow, so much has been happening I hope I can think to remember it all. Of course we are falling more in love with Alaska with each passing day. It is such a fine, healthy land... we really want to become a part of it.

    It feels pretty far from home up here... traveling North for days and days, but still only being in the lower panhandle. Right now we are camping up Petersburg Creek. We arrived in Petersburg late Sunday night, then went clamming on the beach early the next morning with some people we met. We kayaked across the inlet to a cabin as the tide was coming in and fixed clam chowder for dinner.

    Next day we started hiking up the river to camp and do some fishing. Lots of new flowers, new birds and bird calls to learn. Turned out most of the fish, cutthroat, salmon and steelhead have gone out to sea right now (they migrate back and forth in different cycles), so we haven't caught any fish yet. But the guys that are living here, working for Fish and Game, made a big salmon dinner for us the other night from a sockeye salmon they had caught in their traps. That night we saw the northern lights, faint but very real and very exciting. First time for Craig.

    We are on an island here, as is almost everything in southeastern Alaska. There are only black bears here (no grizzlies, fortunately), but they are very shy, and we haven't seen any sign of them. Saw our first bald eagles on the ferry; now they are becoming commonplace. Yesterday one flew within a few yards of us! We did see wolf tracks on the trail... boy, I'm dying to see one of those guys! And yesterday on a day hike up to the lake we saw a beaver.

    There is so much to learn... we seem to fill up with information every day. People are happy to talk and tell us about the life up here: fishing, animals, boats, plants, places... it gets very intense sometimes.

    Today it is raining... that's all it ever does in the southeast.

Glad to finally get the opportunity to write. Moving camp down river to perhaps a better fishing hole.

    Love to all of you, Dena

Next day, a rather elated P.S:
    I caught my first Alaska fish today… it was a Dolly Varden, which is a kind of river-sea trout. Now I feel I have finally arrived! There are whales around here which we see from the ferry and from land… small killer-whale types.
    Tomorrow we kayak back across the inlet to town to catch the ferry for Juneau. This has been really pleasant here. Today was even sunny long enough to sun bathe for a few hours! We're getting pretty ripe (speaking of bathing)… will be nice to take that long hot shower on the ferry.
    Anxious to keep heading North…
    Yea!

    Dena

CHAPTER 2: Happy Homer homesteaders

July, 1974
Homer, Alaska

Dear Kirk,

Thinking about you so much. Would love to hear how things are going lately. This place is all we could have hoped for and more. Hope someday you get around to seeing the North, too.

How goes the motorcycle racing? Craig's brother Kirk is still very into racing, too... except he messed up his knee pretty bad a while back which temporarily put him out of business. I still think your sport is pretty dangerous, but you may think that about skiing!

We're looking for a cabin for the winter now... there are a few good possibilities. The ride here was really crazy... all the way from the time we went from Haines to the Alcan Highway to Homer in the back of a pickup truck.

Great little town, Homer... even a natural food store, hip book store. Stays light here till past one AM, which is when we usually get to bed. Sun sets at 9 or 10 PM.

Things sure are better now that Craig and I are together doing what we both like best. Living apart was definitely not the best thing our relationship has gone through.

Please send Box #1 labeled "Boots" by parcel post immediately.

Much love, Dena

July, 1974
Homer, Alaska

Howdy Folks,

At last some good news... we have finally found a cabin to live in for the winter, and are supposed to move in in a couple days. It's so perfect we can hardly believe it's real. We'll only be convinced after we have been living there a while. It's about five miles from town... up on a ridge that stretches for miles behind the town, toward the head of Kachemak Bay. You have to go along dirt roads and trails to get there.

We are going to build a sled this winter to harness up to in order to haul food in after the snows come. There is a food co-op in town through the book store where you can order 25 and 50 pound bags of organic grains, legumes, seeds, dry fruit, etc. from this place in Seattle. Lots cheaper that way and good food!

The cabin has a really fine wood-burning cookstove (with an oven even!) to cook on. I can't imagine doing it any other way right now... but using a chain saw is cheating a little. So we're going to cut down some dead trees nearby with a two-person cross-cut saw, and chop them up with an axe. There are also big coal deposits here, and you can go gather it on the beach to use for winter heating.

The fireweed is now growing up over Craig's head... the hills are all purple and green... outrageous! We are going to start work in the crab cannery out on the Homer Spit in a week or so. We have applied to work for Fish and Game, but they won't even look at an application till you've been in the state a year, which makes you a resident. We have already gotten Alaska driver's licenses, so we're on our way.

Apparently after you've gotten your residency and have a college degree, it's almost for sure you have a job. So perhaps by next summer we'll be in with Fish and Game. That would be so great!

Oh wow... we just talked to the people who have the cabin. We can move in for sure right away! We're so happy... we really have a home! We want to fix it up and make it even better. Can't wait!

Also, no brown bears in the immediate area, so we are

going to try to get Sol sent up. We went hiking in the mountains across the bay last week (huge glaciers over there). Picked a ton of blueberries, and I made an outrageous blueberry pie… yumm!

You can send up the rest of the boxes now… all but the skis (which we want sent air freight later). Hope it's no huge trouble. So glad you are thinking about how to make it up here. I know it is your kind of place, too. It actually gets hot here in the summer! Hope your vacation was really outasite.

I love you, Dena

August, 1974
Homer, Alaska

Hello again,

We are all moved in to our cabin now. Yesterday we spent giving the place a thorough cleaning and going through. Now it really feels like ours… fresh wildflowers in the windows, beautiful old vertical log walls. The rent is free… the guy who owns it lives up in the Yukon somewhere, and doesn't mind people living here.

There's a lot of work we still want to do on it… build a top to the porch, fix up the outhouse, put in a sink, perhaps build a wood shed, make a divider with shelves (it is only one room now). And chop a ton of wood.

We haul water up from a spring which is only a few yards from the cabin. We are very lucky to have such a good water supply. This winter we will keep a large garbage can type thing inside which we will fill with snow and set by the stove to keep a constant water supply. Very dry year here.

The nearest cabin is a mile away. It's so quiet here, I never want to go into town or to work at the cannery. But we will need a lot of supplies… like a kerosene lantern for light at night. We are also using a green Coleman stove to cook on when we don't want to start a fire. We wash our clothes at the spring… using a tub and some warm water (which is also how we bathe). There is a fine old washboard, the scrub part is even thick glass… which makes it a bit easier.

Anchorage is 225 miles away… a little too close for comfort. As Craig puts it, "The place that has everything you could possibly not want."

Before you send the last box, perhaps you could look in the bottom drawer of my dresser for a large black book entitled *Last Whole Earth Catalog* access to tools, and add it somehow. If you also find one called *Weed Cookbook* send it, too. And read my thesis someday if you ever want to get bored.

For Barb: Thanks so much for the nice letter. Your planned vacation sounds super. Don't worry… I can definitely see the advantages of having a trailer especially after having traveled the way I have for the past few years. I may pick berries for the berry shop in town in return for some preserves. Trouble is… when you pick berries, you want to do something with them yourself! Please send a few cards while you're gone.

Well back to work… lots to do.

Love, Dena

September, 1974
Homer, Alaska

Hello Family,

A quiet day and time to write a letter. We have just got back home a couple days ago from a mad week on Kodiak Island, working to earn the last of our money for winter. We heard the pay was better and one could get longer hours. So, after working 23 days in a row at the cannery in Homer, we went to Kodiak by ferry, worked the 12-hour night shift for seven nights at a crab cannery, and, half-dead, returned to Homer knowing we were set for the winter if we stayed alive to enjoy it.

Yes, Saturday's child works hard for a living! You can bet we'll really lay it on at Fish and Game next spring for a job in the field with one of their research projects. By now we're so sick of seeing crab that we can't imagine why anyone would want to eat the stuff, let alone pay for it. At first we enjoyed eating the crab, shrimp and occasional halibut and salmon. One night I made crab thermidor, and Craig said it was the best crab he ever had.

Fall is really here now... the smell, feel and look of it. The leaves of the fireweed are all bright yellow and red now. I do love it... fall is definitely my time of year. It actually gets dark at night now... in fact the day-length is radically changing. Soon the sun will be gone away to the south, and we will see what this northern living is all about.

Homer itself is so much quieter now... all the Winnebagos have gone back to California or wherever they came from, and people in town are less uptight. Fall is a mellow time. Are you still doing your yoga, Mama? I'm going to get into it more this winter. Right now we're too busy chinking the holes between the logs of the cabin, hauling wood, etc.

Now we feel more moved in than ever. So before you breathe your last sigh of relief, we think we're ready for the skis to be sent. You have been so great about getting all our things sent up here... thanks so much for sending the boxes and all the, uh, little extras. Craig's mom is sending us a grinder, one that grinds fine flour; something we've been needing a long time. I baked my first wood-burning-stove bread the other day… came out better than any I ever made.

Hope Barb and Bruce made it back fine… would love to hear a little news from that end of the world soon. Also, do I still have two brothers or not?!? I often wonder and wish they would get off their butts and write to me! Hey, please?

Hope you make it back to Independence this year. We were there about this time last year. It's so fine… a lot like here, fresh and beautiful.

Always good to hear from you all.

Love, Dena and Craig

October, 1974
Homer, Alaska

Dear Folks,

Well, I'm finally beginning to believe I'm living in Alaska. We just had a little cold spell that gave us a good prelude to winter. The first snow yesterday... it was pretty exciting. That morning I had to break the ice on the spring to get the food out we were keeping there. The brilliant golds and yellows on the nearby cottonwoods have now been blown off by the winds... brrr!

The sun is saying good-by to the North for this year... no more 11 PM sunsets; the days get noticeably shorter each one. Our rough-legged hawk pair is gone, to return in the spring, and only the boreal chickadees and a few others will be with us all winter. Tonight we heard an owl. The annual plants have died back, putting forth all kinds of interesting and artistic seed dispersal mechanisms to gather and make into dry arrangements.

Yesterday nature laid a little meat on our table. I started walking down the trail, when I saw a little blood and marks in the snow. I followed the marks a couple feet, and there was a snowshoe hare lying under a tree with its neck quite broken. We figured out that a coyote killed it and was about to eat it when Sol scared it away (yes! We have Sol now... more about that later).

The hare was in perfect shape, and must have died only minutes before, so while Sol and I watched with interest, Craig carefully skinned and gutted it. We have the fur hanging up now by the stove to dry. It is so soft and warm! Apparently now is the best time of year to eat them, so we seasoned it a bit, and baked it for dinner last night. Very good... and with fresh-picked blueberry muffins for desert. Sol got the liver, lungs and heart which he just loved, needless to say.

When we were down in the forest the other day, we saw a young small cow moose. It wasn't that afraid... just stood there looking as we looked back. It's probably planning to winter here. A nice neighbor.

Lately, we have been putting most of our energy into getting the winter wood. With one person on each end of our cross-cut saw, it's amazing how many trees can be logged, especially as we get stronger. After we cut the dead trees down and into logs, we hoist them up onto our shoulders and carry them the ¼ mile or so up to where we stack them up on end near the cabin. Some are so heavy, we have to carry them together to get them here… whew!

I am also getting into making jams for the first time. There are so many berries here… I have already made several jars of blueberry jam and cranberry jelly from berry patches nearby. Yesterday we picked some crowberries down by the creek after the snow melted. I'm still planning on making some nagoonberry jam and rosehip jelly.

I've never gotten so much satisfaction from cooking before, and I rarely seem to get tired of it. I guess it's because it is in my own home and for my own man that makes it so enjoyable. Craig is convinced I'm a great cook… what a joke! He also does a lot of baking and cooking himself… in fact he makes most of the bread. Lately he has been experimenting with making home-brewed beer which is amazingly simple and very good.

So, we went to Anchorage to pick up our pooky dog, who was jetting up from California. You should have seen it when we got Sol out of that cage… the three of us jumping around, hugging, laughing, weeping and barking. I'm so happy to have him here, but I've never seen him with so little hair. He'd better get busy and make some quick! We are feeding him a lot to fatten him up for the cold days and nights ahead, and I know he's really going to like it here.

While in the city we got a nice guitar and a few songbooks, so now we will have winter music. With my previous experience, I'm already getting better, and Craig is very determined to start learning. We also got some leather, out of which we are going to make mukluks. They are the best way to have warm feet when the snow is dry. Maybe we'll top them with the hare's fur.

I can understand your concern about Craig and I becoming "weary" of one another here, but there are cures for cabin fever. One is love; another is skiing. We are getting together a rather good collection of books to read, I'm in the middle of making some curtains, and Craig is carving wooden spoons. There is a great deal to learn about this place, this way of life, and always wood to be chopped.

We are gradually getting most of the things we need. But if you need Christmas ideas, we would still like having a fair sized pressure cooker for soups and canning. Any ideas on what you guys would like for Christmas?... I'm already beginning to have some good ideas on the subject. Going to town tomorrow to see if the skis are here... will add a P.S. if they are.

    Much love to all, Dena

P.S. The skis just arrived and we have them. Thank you, thank you! XXOO!

November, 1974
Homer, Alaska

Hello All,

It's been snowing for two days now, and our world is turning soft and white. It makes a cozy cabin seem even homier. We always feel more remote and isolated when it snows. The temperature is still only about 32 degrees, however… it seems stuck there.

We just got back from a four-day backpack along the beach and bluffs from Anchor Point to Homer. The first day was so unusual as it was probably the second honest-to-goodness clear day in about two months. We had to plan our beach walking according to the tides, and when the tide was up, we had to climb up into the frozen muskeg and forests above. Many frozen waterfalls and icicle formations on the bluff faces, and snowy peaks across the water. We walked through enough coal to heat our cabin for the next ten years!

The day after we got back this snowstorm started. The snowshoe hares are now the color of the snow. We saw one on a walk in a nearby cottonwood grove… so soft-looking and plump.

Today I'm making roasted/salted soybeans for the first time. Mama, do you have it perfected yet? The second batch of soybeans just came out… they're crunchy! Craig is trying to finish them all off right now.

Now for the question in your letter: Homer is really pretty small, I guess, but growing. They say about 3,000 people, which probably includes people like us scattered around the hills and down dirt roads.

We sent a sample of our future garden soil to Craig's dad to analyze, and he sent back a report telling us we need to add nitrogen and potassium. We were going to put on manure from a neighbor's barn and wood ash from our stove, so that should take care of it.

We have just decided we are going to ski out to town for the first time. In fact, I'm so excited I can hardly write this letter now. Sorry, but I must cut this short… got to go skiing, whoopee!

Love, Dena

December, 1974
Homer, Alaska

Hi Folks,

We've been seeing a lot more of the sun since winter has arrived, ironically enough. The last couple days have been blue, blue skies against the white snow and green trees. It's so welcome... we love it... makes skiing even more fun with lovely views to the mountains across the water.

The sun makes the days seem not quite as short as we thought they'd be. It sets about 3 PM, so if you don't get right up and at 'em, and get something accomplished, you feel like the day just passed you by. The snow outside gets deeper, but our spring is still running if we keep the ice chipped away.

We are getting more and more used to skiing in the dark... especially the afternoons we come home after being in town. With full packs... ugh! That's the part I don't much like. We've recently discovered one sorta good thing that town has to offer... one can go swimming at the indoor pool at the high school once a week for a dollar. It's fun doing laps and diving off the diving board, then walking out into the snow to ski home.

Sometimes when I'm skiing, and it's light, and the snow is new and good, I find myself wishing so much I could take you guys out for a nice gentle ski up on the ridge to look at the mountains and follow the moose, rabbit and ermine tracks. Maybe our local goshawk would fly over.

Our Thanksgiving was very quiet and very nice... my first turkey dinner I've ever made... and out of a wood-burning stove, no less. We baked a little 8 pound turkey with stuffing, served with homemade cranberry jelly, fresh pumpkin pie, and everything in between. Craig passed out, stuffed to the gills, right after dinner (the homebrew he drank before and with dinner may have helped him along!).

Our little Christmas tree is decorated with strings of dried rosehips, bunches of alder cones, candy canes and ornaments I made with cut paper. We almost didn't have a merry Christmas, as we didn't know where Sol was for about 24 hours the other day. Terrifying. He has a habit of going out to chase the rabbits along their little trails through the forest. One evening he didn't come home. We called and whistled, but no Sol, and it was snowing so much that any tracks made were covered in a few minutes, so no use going out to look. We figured he had gotten lost or kicked by a moose, never to be seen again. A rather tense, teary night.

Then, toward the end of the next day, I decided to ski out to look and call, not with much hope. I had only skied out the trail a few hundred yards, when I heard a "quee, quee," and there was Sol under a tree caught in an old rabbit snare (the rabbits set them out for the dogs!). We got him right out and he didn't even seem any less plump than before (he eats like a horse lately).

So now our little family is reunited… even more appreciative of each other than before. A prayer answered. Time to rest now.

Love to everyone, Dena

December, 1974
Homer, Alaska

Dear everybody,

Whew! Christmas is over and time at last to slow down and get to reading and doing all the little projects I've been wanting to get to... and more time for long ski trips!

Your presents were received with delight and thanks. That pressure cooker is perfect. Next fall I'm really going to be busy canning like never before. And I've never seen so many kinds of nuts and dried fruits... we poor hippies feel our humble home flowing with bounty!

I couldn't believe those persimmons, Lee... wow!... that's the last thing I expected to see. I made cookies out of some of them, and yesterday I canned the rest so that we could extend our enjoyment of them over the winter. We appreciated the bay and oregano you sent. It reminds me that California grows more than just smog.

Sol brought in our Christmas turkey on the sled, along with some last minute packages we got. You should see him toiling in the traces... we've been singing, "Sol-ie the red-nosed sled dog" to him. A friend gave us the old sled to rebuild, and it fits Sol perfectly. He's mostly going to help us haul wood and dog food, finally earn his keep!

At last it has been dropping below zero here... just a few degrees, but it's noticed. Time to get out the woolen long underwear. One of the immediate manifestations of zero weather is that the sprouts from alfalfa and mung beans can't even grow inside when it's that temperature outside. If we want sprouts to keep growing, we're going to have to start sleeping with them!

We just got back from our first extended ski trip and snow camping of the season. Skied out to Caribou Lake, 10 miles from the end of a road. Went fishing through a hole in the ice, but didn't catch anything this time. We got to eat some fish, though, with an old guy who lives out there in a cabin by himself, caretaking. It's a beautiful area... the lake itself is several miles long, with nearby hills surrounding it, and high mountains in sight. Not too much wildlife out yet... just a few moose, ermine, snowshoe hare and ptarmigan.

We stayed in our small mountain tent, trying out our new sleeping bags. It got really stormy the last night we were there, leaving a new foot of snow, so we had to break trail all the way out the next day. We were so exhausted and hungry when we got to the truck that we decided to do something very unusual for us. When we got to town, we went out to dinner. By midnight, though, we were back up to the quiet of our hill.

Looks like I'm out of room for now. Please write and tell us some of your goings on.

Love, Dena and Craig

January, 1975
Homer, Alaska

Dear (Grandmother) Ruby, (in Pasadena, California)

I've been meaning to write to you since I got the birthday card from you months ago. Thanks so much. I often think of you and how you said you don't like cold weather. Well, this is definitely not your kind of place! It has been getting down to 10 below zero lately… rather hard to get used to. Fingers and toes get numb even while skiing, ice forms on our eyelashes, sometimes freezing them shut, and we have to wear hats that pull down over our faces.

It's amazing how much more warm and comfortable we feel when the temperature goes up to zero, or even 10 above! All what you get used to, I guess. Today was warmer like that, so we spent the afternoon cross-country skiing. Very light skis, you can go up and down hills with them, through the forest and all.

We like especially looking for the tracks of animals in the snow. There are many moose wintering here… the other day we saw one with a calf. Our most recent discovery was lynx tracks, but we haven't seen the actual animal yet. It is a member of the cat family, very beautiful.

Also many ermine (a weasel that turns white in the winter), snowshoe hare (also turns from brown to white), and more birds than I could list on one page (in the summer, at least). Fortunately, there are no grizzly bears in the immediate vicinity. Also no wolves, though I wish there were… I'd love to see one. Just coyotes around here.

We ski into town about once a week, which is about six miles away down the ridge on the coast. We have a great deal of food here, so we could stay out for months if we wanted to. We just like having fresh food, too, since it's available.

No matter how cold it is, our one-room log cabin keeps us cozy and warm. The wood-burning cookstove is always going (except when we're asleep) with wood we cut by hand. We hope to have a garden this summer, and I'm planning to can a lot more things with our new pressure cooker.

Craig is a really good man to be with… I wish you could meet him.

Much love to you, Dena

P.S. The red things I sent you are rosehips. Steep them a while in hot water for tea. Good and vitamin C!

January, 1975
Homer, Alaska

Howdy Folks,

Can't remember when last I wrote, or what it was about, but guess I'll begin with the little cold spell we had recently. It got down to 18 degrees below zero. Sorta reminded us where we were! You really have to think about what you have on if going out for any period of time... layers of wool, heat socks, boots (and feet) over the stove, pull hats down over our faces till only noses and eyes peek out, then go.

But now the temperature has gone up to over 32 degrees (that's what comes from living on the coast) and we're running around in our shirt sleeves again, having to open the door of the cabin occasionally from getting too hot.

Yesterday we took the longest ski yet... about 20 miles round trip to some of the distant ridges toward the head of the bay. Met an old guy living on a homestead he built. He hasn't been to town since November. That's the way to do it. Then we skied home and I baked some delicious carob brownies... mmm!

Enclosed are some dried rosehips. Make some tea and put lots in. We have so many... one of the few forms of material wealth we have. So to be shared.

The most recent tracks we've seen are those of the lynx, but we haven't seen the big kitty yet. Mostly nocturnal and shy, I guess. Today I saw what is supposed to be a very rare bird here... the northern three-toed woodpecker.

We are melting snow for water finally. The spring is still running, but as it got colder, it froze farther up its course, gradually lowering the level so that we can't dip out of it anymore. Melting snow isn't so bad, as we keep our many-gallon container full here in the cabin. It just ices over on top the nights it gets below zero outside.

We just bought 60 pounds of honey. That's five gallons. And a case of evaporated milk. It's absurd how much food we have here. Fifty more pounds of wheat berries came through the co-op. It's a good feeling to know we could have enough to eat. Especially when the world around us seems held together by whims and pieces of paper.

It's hard to say right now exactly when you should come up, though offhand it seems that summertime when all the wildflowers are out and the long days are here is what you would like. It's not that cold in September, and the fall color is beautiful…

Well, it's just hard to say right now. We are applying for outdoor jobs all over the state, and won't know our summer plans for a while.

Things will fall into place. We want to do some traveling around this spring, too.

Love, Dena

February, 1975
Homer, Alaska

Hullo,

The long-awaited storm finally came, and now the snow is piling up outside more than any storms have given so far. All white on the trees again... yea, it's winter again! We were beginning to wonder.

So I've taken the opportunity to do some things I've been wanting to inside. Today I started, and almost finished, my mukluks. Made from leather and waterproofed canvas. They are very roomy in order that there be a lot of dead air space which is warm and stays between your feet and the cold. They're not quite fur lined with caribou or seal, but I have second best to that in the form of my snuggies... sheepskin (with some wool left on the inside) slippers. I wear them along with a few pairs of socks inside the mukluks.

Every week it seems we send away for things from "Outside," be it tea, tools, clothes, etc. It makes it fun to go to town to see what may be there. We wish most of all, though, to find a couple acceptance letters for work on a fish weir on some stream a hundred miles from noplace.

You can keep sending those newsletters to us if you want. We don't come in contact with much along that line, and Craig seems to consume reading matter about as voraciously as he does food. And they are good fire-starter. You can send the *New Republic*, too... it might be good fire-starter as well.

If you liked the story about the guy who hadn't been to town since November, then here's another one. Did I tell you about the old man living at the head of Seldovia Bay we met last summer? He used to live somewhere in the Interior, and told us that at that time, one spring he came out from wherever he was living to learn that World War 1 was over. He didn't know it even started.

Glad you are satisfied with living in California... it's good to be happy where you are. I guess picking oranges in the middle of January could generate some affinity for a place, to be sure.

So can skiing all day in the crisp fresh air with mountains on all sides. Some of us had to come North... it wasn't even a decision, more a natural evolution. So glad you're at least coming to visit.

Much love, Dena

April, 1975
Homer, Alaska

Dear People,

More and more talk of spring around here. We've been spending a lot of time sitting out on the front porch in the sun after breakfast. A bit of a storm today, though... lucky we didn't leave on a ski trip like we'd planned. Last week we went out for four days, and the second day it started snowing, which meant that on the way back home we had to break trail 15 miles through wet snow a foot or so deep. Thoroughly exhausting, but we felt so good afterwards.

So glad you guys are coming up in September... that's one of the nicest times I remember so far. Lots of color, things are slowed down from summer, and the berries and mushrooms are beginning to ripen. We'll put you to work hauling firewood! I'm pretty sure we'll be here next winter, too, and will be done with our summer work. Mostly what I want to say is be flexible. Once you're on that ferry, you've arrived in Alaska.

As for the aurora, there is no guarantee when you'll see it, although it is most common in wintertime because of the longer hours of darkness. You just have to be out looking at the northern sky after it gets dark. It just all depends on the activity from the sun (sun spots) around that time.

Our spring and summer plans have gone through some pretty heavy changes lately, speaking of being flexible. One position became available on Kodiak Island with Fish and Game, and Craig was hired. Good to know the money will be flowing in again, but it means we will be separated starting mid-May until early September. wow.

Apparently, things are always opening up all summer, so a little persistence should land me something. In a way, things are working out in the best way possible (aside from the part about being away from each other). Now I will be able to start a garden for sure, which will be exciting and gratifying. Since I should be here at least the first part of the summer, I am starting it now.

I have been building flats to start the seedlings in, and today mixed all the soil, manure and wood ashes to get everything ready for planting inside day after tomorrow. Cabbage, broccoli, lettuce, chard, spinach, onions. It's pretty crazy standing outside with five feet of snow all around, and the wind bringing little flurries now and again, but we have high hopes for a beautiful garden. I'm going to have a special row called "Mama's turnip patch."

Love your nice letters, Dena and Craig

June, 1975
Homer, Alaska

Dear Folks and such,

I just got back from a beautiful week on Kodiak with Craig. He is working out on the Karluk River at the other end of the island... a really fine river with a native village at the mouth. He is helping to set up a new fish weir camp. (That's where they trap salmon temporarily to count them as they go up the river to spawn).

He didn't know I was coming and it was fun surprising him. When I landed in Kodiak, I had no idea how I was going to get out to see him... I just knew I had to. Something was with me, though, because when I walked into the Fish and Game office, his boss was just leaving to fly out to see him (no roads to the river, of course).

So his boss and I flew out there in an amphibious plane called a Goose. What a flight... I never realized Kodiak Island is such a beautiful and diverse place. Lots of forests around town, but very open rolling hills on the other side of the island. A few days later we all flew back to the town side of the island, where Craig will be the rest of the summer. Craig has caught four king salmon that he's trying to get smoked for the winter.

I imagine you are feeling the full force of summer coming on by now. What's it like to be hot, anyway? Up here the thermometer has been topping out at 55 degrees... a real scorcher!

My garden is almost all in now. The last couple days I've been working very hard turning over the soil, removing the masses of fireweed roots, and adding all my organic goodies. Yesterday I planted 10 pounds of potatoes, which should yield the beginnings of a winter supply. They do very well in this climate, and need little care, especially since this is looking to be a wet year. Tomorrow everything in the flats goes outdoors. Maybe plant some carrots, too.

Just in time, as I should be starting work for Fish and Game sometime next week. They are flying me out to the island I'll be working on... can't wait. Will write more when I get there.

We didn't make it to Glacier Bay last year, so I don't know too much about it. You can fly in for sure, and I'm sure you can camp there. The ferry from Seattle doesn't go in the Bay. Hope you go there, though… it's supposed to be beautiful when it's clear weather enough to see, that is.

Much love to you all, Dena

July, 1975
Kalgin Island, Alaska

Hi Everyone,

I've been out on Kalgin Island in the Cook Inlet near the Alaskan Peninsula for about a week now, but it seems like so much longer. Fish and Game flew me out here on a Cessna 185 float plane, to the two-mile long lake the cabin is on. During the flight over Cook Inlet, we looked down to see a large group of the white beluga whales swimming below. From that distance, they looked like a mass of maggots, it was funny and exciting. They are truly a rare sight.

I work with another girl counting, measuring, taking scale samples and tagging red salmon (the species that spawns in lakes). We are pretty much finishing up doing the same on the salmon smolt that are leaving the lake to head out to sea for a few years.

We are in the FRED division of Fish and Game which stands for Fisheries Rehabilitation Enhancement and Development. All the various projects we do, and data we collect, are for management of the red (or sockeye) salmon population.

Yesterday we took the skiff out to pull the gillnet we had on a 24-hour set. We mostly got Dolly Varden… a trout… which we dissected and examined the stomach contents of. They are of concern because they eat salmon eggs and smolt (first year salmon); also insects, leeches and larvae. I'll admit it… I'm usually a little green after we finish doing this.

The long days are really far out… it never gets dark… just a late sunset twilight at night. During the darkest time you can still see a couple miles away. Sunset is about 11:30 PM.

Don't worry if sometimes there's a lag in reply time from your letters. We never know for sure when we will get mail planes in and out, so do forbear.

Love you all, Dena

July, 1975
Kodiak Island, Alaska

Dear Doris and Del,

Here's a little taste of the North that should set your mouth watering for more. This was my "first king salmon," a moderately sized fish at twenty-five pounds (crazy, huh?).

King salmon are the largest salmon and also the oiliest and richest. They head up river in spring and spawn in late summer. It's a beautiful, fat, fighting fish when it begins its trip upriver.

Please refrigerate this as soon as possible. Happy eating.

Love, Craig

P.S. Thanks for being such good, understanding pre folks-in-law.

August, 1975
Kalgin Island, Alaska

Dear Folks,

Great news! Craig was able to leave Kodiak and come out to work with me until the end of the season since my working partner had to leave. Things are pretty much the same around here now, and we're beginning to settle into the pace of weir camp life. The salmon run up the river is a record low this year... only a dozen or so come through each day. So we have been mapping the stream, doing velocity studies and various projects to keep busy.

One thing that keeps us busy is undoing the work of beavers on the river. Every day we walk about halfway down the river, and take apart the dams that the beavers build back up every night. They don't seem to appreciate the importance of the salmon being able to pass on up into the lake to spawn.

Another fun job is going across the lake to the shallow spawning beds, and watching salmon mating behavior. They pair up, then work on beating depressions in the gravel beds with their tails, so they can lay their eggs and sperm together, then cover it all up with more gravel. Then they die, rot away and make a stinking mess that provides nutrients in the stream system for the next generation. Nice, huh?

We've been getting some sunny weather again; it almost feels like summertime. We go swimming in the lake almost everyday. I think I'll really miss not living on a lake now... it makes washing clothes and keeping clean so much easier. You should see Sol riding around in the skiff, sitting on the bow, sniffing the breeze. And when we go berry picking, he walks from one to the other of us, begging for berries to be thrown his way.

They might take us off the island in a week or two, and from then until you come we'll mostly be getting the cabin back in shape, and perhaps buying a used pickup. Not so great news: we heard that a mother black bear and her two cubs have moved into our Homer cabin. Supposedly someone saw them lying on the bed, so there may be a lot to do to get it back in shape.

Wow, the time sure seems to be drawing near for your trip all of a sudden, and I feel as though I should be telling you all kinds of things, but I don't know what. Craig says to spend a week in the refrigerator before you leave for Alaska, to acclimate yourselves. Not really... it should be fairly warm here, but possibly a bit wet at times. Raingear makes life more pleasant.

I thought I might clarify a bit for you Craig's and my plans. We are quite serious about getting married in the near future, however, there is a law in Alaska that you can't work together on a state job if you are married. Since we are fairly sure at this point we want to do this same kind of thing next summer, too, we will have to put off any wedding until at least after that.

Hope that sounds good with you all. We'll keep you informed.

For now... Love, Us

October, 1975
Homer, Alaska

Dear Haskells,

Just to let you know we are back in Homer, very anxious to hear from you all that you made it back to California OK. On our recent trip, we saw some magnificent country… approaching real wilderness. The ferry took us through Prince William Sound to the base of the Columbia Glacier, and moved quietly into a herd of a few hundred harbor seals. With the binoculars, their faces were brought close enough to touch, it seemed, and one could see the beauty of each individual's coat. They just floated around on the ice floes, looking up at us. Exciting!

We met up with some friends in McCarthy, and saw some fine, dry country. At our friends' cabin, a short plane flight outside of McCarthy (landing on a very bumpy gravel airstrip), we saw much fresh sign of brown bear, and a huge paw print, claws and all, but didn't see the bear, unfortunately (or fortunately?). We did see some Dall sheep high up the wall of a canyon, though. It's nice to be around so much rock and dry weather… we miss that around Homer.

The bears came back to our cabin, but didn't go in… whew! The feel of winter is approaching, and we seem to be preparing for it with the same vigor as last year, even though we feel much more relaxed about the whole thing. It looks like we are progressing in the direction of comfort… a bad sign perhaps?

We have tarpapered the roof (it doesn't leak anymore!), and insulated the ceiling. Now with the weather in the 30's and 40's, it is usually much too hot in here. Can't wait till the temperatures drop to a comfortable level. You'll also be glad to know we've gotten the steering and brakes fixed on the truck, along with a lube job. Goes better now. Craig even lets me drive it sometimes… nice guy!

Our future plans are quite up in the air at this point. The main priority that both of us feel now is to find a piece of land to put our savings and our roots into. A place to really call home. Land prices are just outrageous up here, but on the other hand Alaska really holds me, and we've barely begun to see it all.

The latest addition to our little family is four Rhode Island Red hens and a Cornish-cross rooster. We decided we wanted chickens a week or so ago, so we got busy and finished the chicken house (remember that half-done small log thing on the way to our spring?). It's neat to be awakened by our crowing rooster in the morning. The four other roosters we butchered ourselves; plucked, gutted… the whole bit. Quite a grisly affair, but it certainly puts one's position on the food chain in perspective. We are keeping them in a friend's freezer in town.

Well, better get some rest for hauling firewood logs tomorrow.

Love to all, Dena

November, 1975
Homer, Alaska

Hello People,

This may be a bit short, as it's getting rather late, but we're going to town tomorrow, and I want to keep in touch. I got Barb's big box of almonds...wow... we love 'em! Tell her I'll be writing soon.

Needless to say, we're really sorry Kirk won't be making it up now, but I understand, I guess. He just missed about two weeks of clear skies here. It's been fantastic. Of course that means that the temperatures have dropped considerably... it was 3 degrees below zero last night... brrr! No snow yet. But if you work hard you stay warm. Besides spruce, we are using alder and birch trees this year, which burn much longer. No chain saw again this year... we do it all with the crosscut or the Swede saw.

We've also been collecting the coal that washes up on the beaches, and driving it in on the hard, frozen roads. We throw it in the stove at night, so the cabin is warmer when we get up in the morning.

We ate the first rooster from those we bought from a local farmer. Neither of us have ever tasted such tender poultry... it seemed to melt in the mouth! To answer your question: we kill our chickens by me holding them (legs tied together so they don't run around after the head is off), and Craig laying the neck across the chopping block and chopping off the head with the axe. The last time we did it, it went a lot smoother than the first. (We didn't get quite so upset, too).

Our hens aren't laying right now (neither is anyone else's). They seem to go through a "slump" just as the weather first turns cold, but should resume again soon. Anyway, they are entertaining, so we like having them around.

I wish I could tell you not to worry about us and our future, but I guess that is the god-given right of mothers to worry. Of course I know how rare Craig is... that's why I chose him. I guess one would have to be the tolerant sort to live with me, huh? But one thing's for sure... life is hardly ever dull for him!

Anyway, if plans continue in the direction of graduate

school, etc., our life will change quite radically, at least temporarily. Then being apart will take a real adjustment at this point. The more we are together, the more important being together becomes.

So much of my ramblings for now. Happy Thanksgiving.

Love, Dena

December, 1975
Homer, Alaska

Hi Folks,

At last it is snowing again! After two weeks of clear, sub-zero weather with snow too thin and icy to ski on, today it's beginning to look promising. It just has to be a white Christmas! Sure hope the big box of presents will be getting to you soon... let me know immediately when it does (as well as another separate box mailed the same time) so I can stop worrying about them.

Our Thanksgiving was quite an affair this year. All the people in our local "neighborhood" got together in one of the larger cabins for a big feast. Everyone brought something to eat and a lot brought guitars and songs. We're going to spend Christmas in our own quiet little way, though, like last year. It's a nice feeling to have created enough of a home to not feel the need to go elsewhere as many people here do at Christmas time.

I'm enclosing this paper on Alaskan federal lands for you to read so you're up on the latest political events here in the "Upper 1" (as opposed to the "Lower 48"). It was given out at a hearing we went to recently in town. Our friend Rob Bosworth (from UC Santa Cruz) came up from Juneau where he is now living, to help explain Governor Hammond's stand. Rob works out of the Governor's office under Bob Weeden... a fairly important job. He is also working on creating Kachemak Bay as a Marine Sanctuary safe from oil drilling. He got to stay with us one night, hiking in with us under the stars and being treated to our homemade hot spiced cranberry liquor. We sure miss not seeing our good friends more often.

The northern lights have been more frequent lately, but mostly rather faint. Homer is still pretty far south to really get them bright. As the sun reaches its southern-most place, we see less and less of it, but are snug and warm and busy as little northern elves preparing for Christmas.

For now...

Love, Dena

February, 1976
Homer, Alaska

Del and Doris Haskell and Family:

We are going to be married.
Your presence will make our celebration more complete.

April 17, 1976
One o'clock PM

At the home of Rev. Dr. Ken Norris
Bonny Doon, California

RSVP as soon as possible:
Dena Haskell and Craig Matkin
Homer, Alaska

March, 1976
Homer, Alaska

Hello All,

Well, two weeks from tomorrow we will be on the plane heading south… hard to believe at this point. Seems like there's so much to do!

Our trip to McKinley was about the best ski trip we've ever had. We were out five days; took the train up from Anchorage and caught it again going back. We skied up Riley Creek about five miles and made a base camp. The snow was shallow enough under the trees so we could have a fine campfire every night. The river was open and running in spots, so we drank fresh water and didn't have to melt snow for cooking.

It snowed, blowed, and was even clear and sunny one day. That day Craig and I climbed a mountain and saw ranges of snow-capped peaks for miles and miles. Wow… made us want to move to the interior mountains. He's even thinking now of applying to University of Alaska in Fairbanks now so we don't have to leave Alaska.

I hope you will want to be in Santa Cruz at least a day before the wedding. We will probably do something like a dinner for both families the night before. And I will most likely want Barb's help on finishing the flower things then, too. This will be the non-legal celebration type wedding with friends and family this spring. Then we will be able to work together for Fish and Game in Prince William Sound this summer, and we're already looking forward to our autumn Alaskan legal wedding.

Tell Kirk I will give him my official "birthday regards" when I get there.

So much for now.

Love, Dena

From Craig and Dena's Wedding – April 17, 1976
Bonny Doon, California

To everything there is a season,
And a time for every purpose under heaven:
A time to be born and a time to die,
A time to plant and a time to reap,
A time to kill and a time to heal,
A time to break down and a time to build up,
A time to weep and a time to laugh,
A time to mourn and a time to dance,
A time to scatter stones and a time to gather them together,
A time to embrace and a time to refrain from embracing,
A time to gain and a time to lose,
A time to keep and a time to throw away,
A time to rend and a time to sew,
A time to keep silence and a time to speak,
A time to love and a time to hate,
A time for war and a time for peace.
(King James Bible)

Love is patient and kind.
Love is not jealous or boastful,
It is not arrogant or rude.
Love does not insist on its own way,
It is not irritable or resentful.
Love does not rejoice at wrong, but delights in the truth.
Love bears all things, believes all things, hopes all things,
endures all things.
Love never ends…
There are three things that last forever:
Faith, hope and love,
But the greatest of these is love…
(King James Bible)

May, 1976
Homer, Alaska

Dear Folks,

At last we are on our way down the Kenai Peninsula and will be in Homer tonight. Spent a day in Anchorage with friends… all of them are into some kind of environmental work. Last evening we went bird-watching at a nearby marsh/wildlife refuge. The migration is really on. We saw trumpeter swans, Canada geese, pintails, shovelers, bufflehead and lots of gulls, of course.

Thanks to brother Lee… we have already made good use of the snow tires you helped us buy. It was snowing like crazy as we went over the first pass after getting off the ferry in Haines. Thanks so much for that and just for being there for our joyous event. I still can't believe how understanding the whole family was about our different way of doing things.

The days are getting very long already… at 10:30 PM it's still light. Good to be back in familiar country, but still feeling those pangs of homesickness for family.

Soon we will be on another ferry going toward Cordova to work together for Fish and Game. We're so excited about being out in Prince William Sound on a red salmon stream for three months.

We'll keep in touch.

Love, Dena, Craig and Sol T. Dog

CHAPTER 3: FALLING IN LOVE WITH PRINCE WILLIAM SOUND

> Father's Day, 1976
> Eshamy Lagoon,
> Prince William Sound

Dear Daddy,

 Well, here I am far away, as usual. The draw of this land on me is so strong, but sometimes it makes me sad that it takes me so far from the ones I love. As we were coming back to Alaska I kept asking myself, "Why am I leaving a place where the sun is shining and flowers are growing, and going to a place where the snow hasn't even melted off the gardens yet?"

 Don't know if that can be answered completely… but there is something of a challenge in the day-to-day work here that makes one feel strong and free. And there is a pervading depth to living so close to those things… the sea, the mountains… that are so much larger than oneself.

 I hope your day today was nice and shared with loving people. You're so lucky to have Mama.

 I wish we could do something to help the fish. The run in the Eshamy River has diminished considerably over the years, and it makes me feel so helpless. The red salmon run this year hasn't begun here yet, so we have mostly been setting up the weir, planting the garden, and exploring.

 Today we kayaked up the lagoon to the base of a mountain, then climbed the ridge to the top of the mountain. I was thinking about you a lot. We could see mountains rising up all around, and inlets down below leading into Prince William Sound beyond. Already I can tell we will become quite attached to this place.

 We've been here two weeks now without a food or mail flight in yet. I don't know how much longer it will be before this letter goes out. Write to us anyway! We miss you.

 Love, Dena, Craig and Sol

June, 1976
Eshamy Lagoon,
Prince William Sound

Dear Kirk,

Well, here we are. How can I describe this place to you? It is without a doubt the most beautiful place I've ever lived. The river flowing out front, salmon jumping in the cove, and endless lakes, mountains and lagoons to explore. Every time we do something really neat I wish you could be with us… just to show you another reality.

What is happening with you now? Are you working? Write me and tell me what's going on. One way or another, maybe after you work for awhile, you have to come up here. We will be at Eshamy for sure until September 15, maybe longer. No excuses this time, OK? Just do it. What is your address?

This afternoon we kayaked out the lagoon a ways. Found a new stream and more wildflowers. The other day as we were coming back from the mouth of the bay in the skiff (18 horse outboard), we came across a murrelet (small duck-like bird) that couldn't fly or dive away from us. Craig picked it up out of the water, and it just sat there shivering in his hands. We didn't know what to do to help it, so we just put it back in the water, and have never seen it again.

Everything I planted in my garden has germinated. With the last straight week of hot sunshine things are growing like crazy, and it is beginning to look like a living place now. Of course, the turnips are biggest of all. Someone in the past planted rhubarb at one side, and the leaves are getting huge.

We finally got it together to climb Eshamy Peak… crossing sloping snowfields and scrabbling up rock and alders to get to the top. It was so insane once we got there… ocean, islands and lagoons in one direction and endless mountains and glaciers in the other. This place blows me away!

Anyway, it would mean so much to me to see you again soon. (They even send us meat out here, not just vegetables!). This is an official invitation to come… try to figure out a way. Get it together and get up here!

Love from all of us, Dena, Craig and Sol

July, 1976
Eshamy Lagoon,
Prince William Sound

Dear Mama and Daddy,

It was so good to get your letter last week. Between the time we left Homer, came out here, and started receiving mail, a month had elapsed since we had seen any at all. It's funny how important mail becomes out here. Even though we feel this place has everything we could want, we still think wistfully about the folks in the outside world.

It is our job to maintain the weir, and count the fish as we let them through. I saw a river otter up quite close the other day. I was standing on the weir, and all of a sudden the fish started scurrying around, going crazy. Then I spotted the otter diving and turning his long, sleek body in the rushing water. He didn't see me, and swam right up to the weir within a few feet of me. Wish I could touch him.

Yesterday while out kayaking we found a sunny hillside with all kinds of flowers. What a delight after being so flower-starved up here. The neatest thing was the wild irises... just beautiful purple things. There were also yellow *Potentilla*, shooting stars, chocolate lily, star flowers, yellow and purple violets, tiny white orchids that smell heavenly. Making the most of the long, endless days.

Well, we almost had a major disaster here a few days ago. We went out to go kayaking, and realized we had not seen the Klepper for at least a day... it was just flat out gone. We jumped in the skiff and went searching. Finally, at the far end of the lagoon we saw it, sitting up at high tide line on a beach just next to the opening of the lagoon. I guess we must have forgotten to tie it up just once, and it went out with the tide.

So yesterday we went on a long trip with it out of the lagoon and into the bay. Near the entrance to the lagoon, a humpback whale surfaced and blew a couple of times before throwing up its flukes and disappearing into the world we cannot enter. Seeing whales close up has become one of our latest endeavors. If Craig sees one, his day is made. It was particularly exciting one day last week while out in the kayak, we saw several whales spouting and heading rapidly into the lagoon toward us.

The first to go by was a false killer whale, a small all-black whale that mostly eats fish. Then we saw a group of three large male killer whales coming after it. It looked as though they were being pushed in slow motion up out of the water, making a whistle, then releasing their air with a sound like rocks rolling down a mountainside. At this point, thinking we were about to witness some kind of a blood bath, I wanted to head for shore. So Craig dropped me off, and he headed back out toward the whales.

It soon became evident they were not intending to kill the other whale. As they all milled around together, another group of four smaller killer whales came up and stayed together off to one side… most likely the females and young. Craig was in the kayak between the two groups as they all joined up, but they completely ignored him. They milled about on the surface, touching and obviously communicating their next move among themselves, then arching and blowing in unison, they all headed back out of the lagoon. Craig was ecstatic, I was shaken. They are powerful and fearless animals!

Love to you, Dena

August, 1976
Eshamy Lagoon,
Prince William Sound

Dear Folks,

    Thank you so much for the pictures… they are some of the best yet, and we look at them again and again with delight. I hope our next wedding is half as lovely. Getting married is so fun, I think we'll do it periodically from now on!

    More and more black bears are appearing, despite the fact that Sol chased the first one up a tree… bad news! Yesterday we watched a yearling bear climbing all over the weir trying to catch a fish. Finally it made a wild pounce on one that was already dead, and proudly climbed up onto the bank and into the forest to eat it.

    In fact, yesterday was a good day for seeing animals. At breakfast we looked out the window and saw the river otter diving and eating something from the bottom of the cove. He is so sleek and cute… I really want to make friends with him, but Sol does his best to prevent that.

    Later, while hiking up a stream doing surveys for pink salmon, we saw two little minks running along a log, seeming oblivious to us. We want to go back there and watch them for a long time. They appear to be denning there. I don't see how anyone could trap them for their pelts; they are much more beautiful in life. At the lake a little farther up, we saw a great blue heron and a loon.

    Back in our own cove, we watched the harbor seal that comes in the evenings to chase the salmon. Sometimes he lies on the bottom looking like a rock while the fish swim above him, but we have yet to see him catch one.

    The blueberries are starting to get ripe now. I've been canning them like crazy lately, and will probably make jam with the next batch. Today I canned some kelp pickles from bull kelp we gathered in the bay. I'm also trying pickled salmon from a recipe a friend gave me… it's a month-long process, and a very safe way to can salmon.

    As the salmon run peaks, so do the numbers of sport fishermen on the weekends. But the beauty of the place is that when they all finally leave in their boats on Sunday and we clean up what they have left behind, we feel the quiet hugeness surrounding us more than ever, and we see all the animals again. And when we climb up the mountains where no one ever goes, or kayak in the still lagoon, it seems hard to believe anyone else was ever here.

Or there are still the times like when we were out in the bay with the skiff and a group of Dall's porpoise came swimming all around us. One of them stayed right with us, zooming along within a foot of the boat, then going up in front of the bow and spraying us as it rose to breathe.

Well, life goes on, and this summer must come to an end. The garden is so lush now, and we are eating out of it at last. I love having it there and will miss it so much when we go. We will have to eat everything up by mid-September. If the fish are still running up the river, though, we might get to stay longer. We sent you some salmon we smoked… hope you got it. We like it best on pizzas.

Love, Dena

September, 1976
Eshamy Lagoon,
Prince William Sound

Hello again,

    We only have a little more than a week left at Eshamy. Hard to believe. Sometimes it seems as if we've always been here and always will be. I just take it for granted that I'm here... having mountains to climb, a river flowing out the front door, and the kayak to jump into at a moment's whim.

    Sometimes I think going back to civilization will be quite a jolt, but I like changes, and flying to Cordova and traveling north will be something new. We want to spend a couple weeks in McKinley Park watching the animals before the snows close all the roads. Then on to Fairbanks and ??? You can keep writing us through Fish and Game in Cordova until we know where we'll be up there.

    True to form, the weather has really deteriorated this past month. We've had a lot of rain, but in the last week or so it has been very peaceful. Hardly any fishermen come anymore, partly because of the storms and partly because almost every fish is up the river. The red salmon run exceeded everyone's expectations, higher than it's been for years. Most of the pink salmon streams around the lagoon have done well, or at least it seems so to us.

    A couple weeks ago we really had a storm... different from mere summer drizzle, something that said, "Fall is here!" Boy oh boy, the wind blew like crazy, and the rain was so hard it seemed ready to come right through the roof. Really exciting. It reminded me of a saying that Laurel and I invented years ago: "One nice thing about bad weather is that you have it all to yourself."

    But on the beautiful sunny days, we try to take advantage of them. One day we took off in the kayak, went down the coast several miles to a bay that connects with Eshamy Lake. Only a short portage over a hill between them, so we carried the kayak over, and were able to kayak all around huge Eshamy Lake. It has a couple long arms to it that took several day trips to explore. While picking blueberries on a tiny island in the lake, we found a single loon egg that had never hatched... huge and brown.

Another day we climbed up a spectacular granite ridge. I hadn't seen that much granite since leaving California.

The bears have been the source of much interest and entertainment lately. There are about nine of them (including a mother and two cubs) that come to fish at the weir. We've named them all, and they seem to tolerate us quite well. The only uncomfortable time was when one bear was fishing off the weir on one side, another bear was eating a fish on the other side, and another was up the trail a ways waiting for a turn. We were standing on the middle of the weir, and at that point we decided it was time for a walk!

Right now we are madly trying to eat up the garden before we leave. We can take the root crops with us, but we've been eating greens every day for lunch and dinner. One man who came out here told me it was the biggest garden he'd ever seen at Eshamy in all the years he'd been here. Guess all that work was worth it.

For now, Love, Dena

September, 1976
Prince William Sound

Dear Family,

　　We are on the ferry now, heading toward Valdez and points north. Leaving the Sound and the ocean… oh, gee. We were just watching some Dall's porpoise go by… it was so terrific getting to know them better this summer. You can bet I'll try my darndest to be in as fine a place next summer in case you are able to come up. We are beginning to get excited about how different it will be in the mountains of the interior. Less moisture!
　　Craig is getting more excited about graduate school at the University of Alaska in Fairbanks since he has decided he wants to study marine mammals, killer whales in particular. He wants to do his field work in Prince William Sound, so we'll be back.
　　It was pretty nice the week we were in Cordova… although a lot of rain, we did some hunting and fishing and saw a lot of birds heading south. Geese, sandhill cranes and all kinds of ducks go through there. Seems there is so much life now… it's just that time of year.
　　I'm sending a small package to you with a taste of our garden in it. Root crops didn't quite attain the size of last year's garden in Homer, but still so good. Hope you enjoy it.

　　My love to you, Dena

CHAPTER 4: Cordova and Cape Espenberg letters

> May, 1977
> Cordova, Alaska

Dear Dena, (at Cape Espenberg, Alaska on Arctic Circle)

We are back in port but there is no one to greet me. Sad! Oh well, it may be a long summer but I am sure we will manage. Builds character.

This fishing period was not quite so busy and we were out until Wednesday. It was a lot of fun, though; I had time to do some bird-watching and beachcombing. Saw a big group of black brant and many mixed groups of shorebirds… even saw a group of Baird's sandpipers, also knots, dunlins, western sandpipers and whimbrels. Also saw a big group of surfbirds out on Shag Rock. I watched nesting pigeon guillemots out on the Whiteshed cliffs.

It's really a rather pleasant work situation… the only hang is the low pay. Only $50 a day, and so far I've averaged about 12-hour working days! Oh well, good experience and I am talking around about a seine job. I am getting used to working on the rolling deck of a boat so don't worry, I'll be fine.

The weather has been great here… light winds and only one day of rain in the last week. Our halibut fishing has been slow, but we just went out and picked our crab pots this morning and got about 40 Dungeness crab. Really makes you glad to be on the coast. I am already looking at skiffs and am told they may be selling dirt cheap this fall.

I am dying to be out chasing whales, etc., on the western side of the Sound. Spring migration seems to be about over, mostly whimbrel and sanderlings around.

I really miss you a lot already. I think it is worse right at first (I hope!). Enjoy yourself and just pretend I am there with you. Hope all is well.

Love, Craig

June, 1977
Cordova, Alaska

Dear Dena,

How is my biologist wife? I hope you are enjoying yourself and making many new discoveries. Today, fortunately, we have been busy so I haven't had time to miss you as much as usual… but I am making up for that now. Down here things have slowed considerably… in fact so slow many of the gillnet fishermen have quit fishing the Flats and are waiting for Coghill and Bering River and Eshamy to open.

We are doing a lot of sitting, which doesn't set well with me at all. When I don't work constantly I just think about missing you and of all the other things I could be doing. I haven't got a seining job for sure yet, but there are several possibilities… hopefully in western Prince William Sound. In the meantime I am collecting and identifying peoples' fish caught incidentally… sharks, skates, flounder, walleye pollocks, sturgeon poachers and a wealth of other weird forms that are new to me. And of course we eat them all (at least taste them). Last night we had dogfish (a type of shark) and it was really good.

I am still getting information on seals, sea lions and whale sightings. All the killer whale sightings I have been told of and I haven't seen one yet this year! Today one of the fishermen brought me a whole harbor porpoise that drowned in his net and I did a dissection and got the skull for science. Fascinating animal on the inside as well as outside, but certainly most beautiful when alive in the water. I am getting a reputation among the fishermen as a marine mammal nut!

Someone from US Fish and Wildlife suggested I apply for a position as a marine mammal biologist assisting with field work on sea otters in Prince William Sound and the Aleutians for six months out of the year (the other six would no doubt be in Anchorage). The field work sounds fascinating, but the thought of Anchorage turns my stomach. I really like the Cordova scene. What do you think?

The weather has been amazingly good… only one small blow since we started gillnetting and a lot of sun. I just wish it was moving faster so I didn't have so much time to think about you.

Boy, it's going to be a long summer! Last night I dreamed that we got married again. It was really a neat dream and I didn't want to wake up.

I will send some fish to your sister for her birthday. I am just about to send a box of Dungeness crab down to my parents. Very few sandpipers around but many nesting phalaropes, mallards, scaups, wigeon, loons and, of course, the Canada geese out on the flats… I did a quick survey when I had an evening off.

I hope you are enjoying yourself, but am also hoping you are lonely for your lover, like I am. See you in the Sound in August (only weeks away).

Love you very much

Love, Craig

June, 1977
Cordova, Alaska

Dear Dena,

Fishing has slowed even more, and we are in town a day early. I kayaked on the lake last evening and today went out on the Copper River flats and chased yellowlegs, dowitchers and phalaropes (or vice versa). Hope I got some good pictures… they all are cheeky buggers. Walking down the banks of the Alaganik is a real treat. Shooting stars, maroon *Pedicularus* and a host of other flowers. The Canada geese have evidently hatched out their young… I saw three pairs, each with seven goslings, on the river.

Things go smoothly, but the fishing is slow and that is not good for my mental frame. It makes me lonely and feel like I am stagnating and not working toward any goal (except the pursuit of money) if we aren't busy.

I am very anxious to plunge into something and really do it… the problem with tendering is it is sort of on the fringe looking at people who are really doing it… the fishermen. I sure admire their independence and the fact that they are running their show. Working for someone else gets very old for me.

I also think a lot about our relationship, being a better husband and giving you more. Certainly a different perspective when separated by 1,000 miles! I am optimistic and think the separation will have its value if I can always remember how lousy it is not to have you with me!

Some problems revolve around my need for a self-run and directed project, but much of it has to do with my attitude and my self-doubt. Well, I am working on it. Do you want to be a fisherman's wife? I would love to combine the fishing and the biology. Sometimes I feel pretty green around here in the fishing world, but something about it is damned appealing.

Cordova is a funny place and I don't know that many people yet and I am lonely as hell, but it will be very hard to leave, I think. I hope you can make it down in August. Until then, do a good job and come on down ASAP.

Love my baby
Craig

June, 1977
Cape Espenberg, Alaska

Dear Craig,

It's about time I wrote in the chance that a plane might happen along one of these days to bring and pick up mail. It's been three weeks yesterday since I've been here, and more like a month since I kissed my baby goodbye.

Guess what? The sea ice went out today… what a delightful surprise to wake up this morning and look out to see water instead of ice. We have been hearing booms and crashes of ice breaking and falling; and seeing ridges of ice building up along leads. It was all in large floating cakes yesterday, and today there are only a few left. The wind has been strong, which helped to break it up.

The sun is out strong all the time now, though it's sometimes foggy on the beach. It gets close to freezing each night even though the sun is shining above the northern horizon all night. We've had one really hot day so far, and that day the bugs came out, so I didn't even mind when it got cold again.

What a land… what a crazy land this is. I'm continually amazed people live here all the time. What is it like now in the land of trees and people, fishes and whales? I feel like I'm on an island… my reality is birds flying, calling, singing, swimming, sitting on eggs, jumping off nests, playing games with me, with each other, and trembling in my hand.

I sure do miss you, sweetheart. How can I write down the wonders that are commonplace, or explain the realization of the perfect tight order in all that embody life here on the Arctic Circle for these few short months?

I finally saw a king eider the other day! Males in breeding plumage are rather rare here, but one day there it was, landing on a nearby lake. Craziest-looking darn bird I ever saw… now why would they go to all that trouble?

Right after that, I saw one of the arctic foxes… it had changed to summer garb now. Black face, legs and feet, and a black patch extending across the top of the rump. Otherwise white. No foxes seem to be denning here this year, which is rather too bad.

What a welcome sight… the flowers are beginning to come out now, the mosses and grasses turning green around the lakes and sloughs. The pink *Peducularis* was about first with the yellow *Potentilla*. Some marsh marigolds in ponds, tiny *Rubus*, Labrador tea and crowberry flowers, and even some fireweed in spots.

The beauty here is in the closer look, and appreciation through understanding. The overall superficial look of the tundra is bare. Without the birds it would seem like there is nothing.

There are three main study plots we are concentrating on. I work Plot 3 mostly by myself, finding nests, marking them, weighing the eggs, and plotting locations of nests on a map. Also I've been nest-trapping semipalmated sandpipers, longspurs and dunlin to band them, measure bills, wings, and weigh them.

This job has been a terrific challenge for me in so many ways. A lot to get used to all at once. There is so much that needs to be done, and I have to learn and figure out most of it on my own.

For instance, one of the most difficult things for me was trapping the birds, and I knew I had to do it. The trap that goes across the nest when sprung is a small circle in which a nylon mesh net is strung. Well, the birds get caught in this net, and one must free them without breaking a wing, leg, or harming them in any way. I am still learning, and hopefully soon it will cease being as traumatic for me as it is for the bird!

And then there are the jaegers. The first time I tried to find a jaeger nest, I was in for a real surprise. The closer I got to where I thought it was, the louder they screamed, did broken wing displays, and finally started dive-bombing me. When I looked up to see this black-masked bird coming at me with black claws outstretched, I let out a yell, stumbled backwards and sat down in the marsh while it swooped up again. That was enough for me, though, and I never did find that nest. What a pair. How ironic it is that they destroy the nests of others, but freak out when they think something's out to get their nest. The villains of birdland.

A couple days ago our "neighbors" came egging on the cape. A native family (reindeer herders from Shishmaref) lives a few miles down the cape in summer. They started gathering eggs in one of the plots, but left when they realized we were working there. About this time of year they have their annual reindeer roundup. They cut off the antlers while still in velvet, which they sell to the Koreans, who grind the antlers into powder for aphrodisiacs. Wild, huh?

Well, I really should end this epistle soon so I get some sleep. The sun is getting brighter. We might start working at night soon when the days get hot and buggy. Now we get going about 9 AM, and work until about 10 PM. Not much time for much of anything else. Usually when I come in from working I'm so hungry I'll happily eat anything!

We all get along pretty congenially, but my guitar is at present my best friend. Whenever I'm feeling a little lonely it is so nice to play and sing… then I feel a lot better.

Well the ptarmigan are a-bageling
The hour is getting late
Here it is the breeding season
And me without my mate!

I miss you
Send some love to live on

Dena

June, 1977
Cordova, Alaska

Dear Dena,

Oh, for the good old days when we were together at Eshamy (or together anywhere). I thought it would be easier to be without you, but it only gets harder! A month from now I should be a wreck! And two months? I may be in the gutter. My only consolation is that many of the fishermen are in the same boat, and have left wives elsewhere and are miserable, too.

Everyone is trying to convince me to become a fisherman... if I stayed around Cordova long I would be. It's a real buyer's market for skiffs. For about $4,000 I should be able to get a fine boat with a good engine.

We had a storm last time out and did some rocking and rolling, but it was fun... just wish the fishing would pick up as it has been slow.

Well, looks like good news; while we were out today, Pete Islieb had a message sent out that he wants to talk to me about seining with him. If it works, it's money in the bank as he is a "highliner," of course. Seining is starting two weeks early as Uncle Ralph says there are already many fish in the creeks. That means day after tomorrow I will be off the Flats and into Prince William Sound... all right! There are about 3,000 pink salmon in the boat harbor and people are catching them off the docks... hopefully a sign of a good season.

I really love being out on the water, but need a fishing partner. How about it? The fishing scene is tough and competitive but so much more real than University b.s. If I could combine fishing with marine mammal research and you, I'd have it made. Sure wish you were here. I think I would like to stay through September 15 so I could duck hunt, fish, and we could mess around.

I am getting used to the smallness of Cordova... it's the size town I could see living near. Wish there was some land available in Prince William Sound.

I walked on Egg Island the other day and found small fuzzy speckled gull chicks hiding in the grass and goslings running through the brush that were almost knee high. Great.

Mostly the weather has been very good. If I work with Pete we should be able to do Hawaii and get a boat!

I miss my baby

Love, Craig

July, 1977
Cape Espenberg, Alaska

Dear Craig,

At last! Letters from you! Yesterday I was having a day off for the first time in about two weeks, and was getting ready to take a bath, when, what do you know, a plane with mail finally landed. It is so good to know you are all right, things are falling into place, and that you've been hurting as bad as I have. I guess I don't even have to tell you how I've been feeling... you said it all in your letters.

Maybe we will think twice before being so nonchalant about a long separation again. I do believe in the end this is a Good Thing we're doing now, but I also know it ain't livin!

Everything you're doing sounds so neat. I realize more and more that Prince William Sound is where I want to call home. Gosh, I wish there was land we could buy over on the western side. The fishing thing appeals to me in many ways, too. I really respect a life made from physical work, and I also recognize the need in our lives for doing some meaningful research. And both would be ideal. If you want to be a fisherman, then I want to be a fisherman's wife.

But if you decide to buy a boat, please try to wait until I can come and help with the decision. You need the esthetic opinion, you know. I had a feeling you would get on seining with Pete Islieb... it was the most logical thing.

The job possibility of working with sea otters sure sounded interesting. It's a terrific opportunity, but on the other hand, you know what my reaction to living in Anchorage is. Right now I want so badly to be really centered somewhere. A place to go out from and come back to... that log cabin home in the sky.

Well, we sure will have a lot to talk about when we're together again, but the sweetest thing I can think of right now is to have my arms around you and not say a word. Time for some sleep now... I wish it was with you...

A couple days later

It's evening again, and I'm sitting in the dunes on the south side of the cape watching what appears to be an empty fox den. How exciting! There are new scats in front of it, so I'm supposed to observe it for four hours to see whether or not anyone is home... i.e. pups coming out to play, or an adult coming back with something to eat.

So far, nothing, which isn't surprising. We don't think any of the foxes here are denning with pups, but about a week ago we saw a red fox for the first time this year... wow, such a beautiful animal. More filled out than the arctic foxes, and a very nice-looking sandy and reddish-brown coat.

There are at least two arctic foxes around, and they have shed out into their black and white summer pattern, making them look pretty thin (very small) and scruffy. I saw both of them at one time on my last Predation watch. We have a blind set up on the edge of Plot 1, and every few nights from 6 to 10 PM, I sit in it and write down what kind of predation takes place in the Plot... jaegers, gulls, foxes, etc.

When the foxes come in, the arctic terns and Sabine's gulls dive-bomb them like crazy, but it doesn't do any good. The foxes just munch down shorebird and tern nests to their hearts' delight, and carry away waterfowl eggs one by one and cache them a little ways away. Those arctic foxes are always on the move. Running along with their mouths wide open, they seem a bit crazy.

Wow! A red fox just appeared...

Later

Well, true to fox form, it appeared, then disappeared just as quickly (into a hole on the other side of the dune, I presume), leaving me wondering if it was a dream or not. Maybe that means there really are pups in there... that would be so neat!

Today it rained for the first time, making me realize how much I like rain and how much of a desert this place is. There were only a couple little showers, but it made everything look so green and pretty. I think because the land itself is actually starting to look alive and I am feeling more familiar with it, this place is starting to grow on me.

When it's hot and I sit and watch something, the mosquitoes have a party on top of my head-net. Then an ice-cold wind can come up and blow them all away. There seems to be no in-between here... this is a cape that knows only extremes.

The sea ice still is visible... the main pack holding about a mile offshore, with a few small chunks closer in. Out in the bay on the south side, we've been chasing isopods and watching them release their young. Also counting and collecting euphausiids.

I often have trouble getting to sleep at night, even though we work 10-12 hours a day. What with the sun shining on the tent all night, but mostly because I can't get used to sleeping alone... especially when it's cold. So I stay up half the night writing letters to you! Everything is so real and so unreal all at the same time. And through it all, there is nothing in the world that means more to me than you.

Next day

It looks like this letter is becoming a journal. We have been working very steadily and at all sorts of odd hours since about the middle of June, as I imagine you have, too. The peak of the birds' nesting season is now passing, and things should start to slow down soon. Now most of the birds have been trapped and banded, and a great percentage of the nests have hatched. When the chicks come out, we band them, too. This is my favorite part so far, I think. I love holding the little chicks... they are all sooo cute! Great big long legs and fuzzy little bodies.

I can't wait to eat wild and pure food again. There is a total lack of fresh vegetables out here, so I have started sprouting the lentils. A plane is supposed to come at the end of next week, and we may get some fresh stuff then.

I think it would be great to spend a month in Cordova doing fun stuff. I'll stay there as long as you want to! Well, now the only dream I have is seeing you again soon.

All my love is for you...
Dena

July, 1977
Cordova, Alaska

Dear Dena,

Well, as of tomorrow it means only about six weeks until I see you. That's about how long I was out at Karluk (I think)… hardly any time at all.

I could write a book about all that has gone on in the last week… my first week of seining. I am beginning to learn what fishing is all about. Not much slack fishing with Pete Islieb… we hit it pretty hard. This early run (two weeks early) isn't real strong yet but we have caught 7,000 + fish and I will have made a little over a thousand dollars for the week. Hard work, long hours (up at 4 AM and to bed at 11 or 12 PM!).

Pete is a real fisherman and our crew on the *Murrelet* is hard working and serious about fishing, but blessed with a fine sense of humor. At first it was tough as I am the only "green" member of the crew (haven't seined before) and I take orders and take the blame for occasional screw-ups; but I am getting the hang of things and we have a good rhythm going and I am beginning to feel pretty comfortable about things.

The weather has been sunny and warm and seas calm. It is great to be back in Prince William Sound… just fantastic country! We watched a group of 6 to 8 killer whales feeding on pink salmon the other night and, needless to say, I nearly jumped out of my shorts. Too dark and choppy for any pictures, although the one large male had a very distinctive dorsal fin. Saw them again the next morning… when they left I was dying to take off and follow.

I am very tired and ready for a break. I am going to stay with the boat over the weekend out here in Port Fidalgo while everyone else flies to town. I don't really know what to say other than I love you and miss you and am even more thankful I have you.

Love, Craig

July, 1977
Cape Espenberg, Alaska

Dear Craig,

A plane just came, bringing us visitors and taking my last letter to you. Three people on OCS funding from the University of Washington will be doing benthic sampling for a few days. It's pretty amazing when you think of how many projects like this are going on all up and down the coast. What will it all come to, I wonder? Well, good jobs anyway for now, and maybe funding for you next year.

It is also amazing what we are already learning from this bird project. Since they have been leg-banding birds and collecting data on nesting behavior here for the past couple years, this year they discovered that some of the same pairs of shorebirds are coming back to the same nest site together to breed and raise young again. And this is after migrating to South America for the winter, then migrating back here in the summer.

Only a month more to go... four short weeks! We've been working pretty hard still, but the peak is definitely over. The last few days I've been working out on Eider Island having a good time. The island is in the middle of a fairly good-sized lake, so we row out there in a tiny inflatable rubber raft. There are about 300 nests on the island, and we had to map them, write locations, check hatching stage the eggs were in, etc., etc.

Some of the little ducklings were already out, and of course are adorable and so fun to hold. If it weren't for the nesting arctic terns on the island chasing away the jaegers and gulls, the common eiders wouldn't be nearly so successful there. I banded some of the tern chicks as the parents dive-bombed me and screeched.

The other day we took the raft across the bay to the south, collecting invertebrates in the mud, and counting the birds. On the way back, we saw a red fox chasing an arctic fox along the beach. The funny thing was, that when the red fox would stop, the arctic fox stopped running, too, then the chase would resume. Very interesting relationship they must have... the little arctic fox must be pretty sure it can outrun its larger cousin.

Sure hope to hear from you by the next mail plane. We are

supposed to do an aerial survey in two days, so I hope that brings letters. Time seems to be going faster... an odd thing to want for a sunny summer, but I just really want to see you!

The sun actually goes below the horizon now... uh, oh!... winter's coming! Time to snuggle. Hope you're sending good vibes to Sol, too... poor guy, I hope he's happy in Fairbanks. I will be so glad when we're a little family again.

I guess when you love and admire someone as much as I do you, it is hard to understand how they could have real self-doubt that would keep them from doing anything they wanted. One thing I think is essential in bringing two people closer together, is having something in common that both are working towards or living for. Sometimes I think you and I are so busy establishing our self-hood that we forget to direct energy toward a dream we share. We won't get anywhere unless we work at it together with as complete trust as we know how.

Sure do miss you

Love, Dena

July, 1977
Cordova, Alaska

Dear Dena,

It is one of those sunny, clear days in Prince William Sound, and another 18 + hour fishing day. Things are going fairly smooth, we are becoming a tight crew with fewer mistakes and foul-ups.

Working for Pete Islieb is interesting. He is a tough fisherman and sometimes is a bit tense. He is really out to make money, of course, has quite an ego and can be very competitive, but can be a good guy when relaxed after fishing.

We have made several new killer whale sightings. We often see them where the salmon are thickest. We have pulled up all sorts of interesting fishes in our net, including a 250 pound salmon shark.

It's time to make another set...

Later

Today we flew into town to re-supply and I gained a little perspective on this crazy scene by reading your letters. Things are wild here... people scrambling to make the almighty dollar, and I am embroiled like the rest. I have already made over $4,000 in less than three weeks. Hardly a moment to sit back, relax and think.

Seining is pretty crazy, repetitive, but lucrative. It is a competitive scramble of sorts, and Pete, of course, is highly competitive. We continually make sets... that is let out the net, purse it up and then haul it in. It is a complicated operation with much power equipment, a maze of lines and net and continual activity. At times it gets a bit monotonous, but it is great to be out working hard and exciting when we catch a lot of fish. I can see gillnetting as a much more interesting and varied fishing technique... with the best part that you are your own boss.

It gets tougher all the time without you and I continually feel the pangs of loneliness. I hope you make it down in time to do a kayak trip in August. I will be about ready for a vacation. Five days a week, about 20 hours a day takes it out of you! Sometimes I don't know if making money in quantity has any positive aspects, but maybe I will think differently later.

The other day we caught a young of the year marbled murrelet in our seine. We kept him for a while… he was a cute bugger. The oystercatcher young are doing their first experimental beachcombing and foraging on the rocks. The adults are very protective and entertaining as they chase sandpipers and other birds away.

I hope some of the love you asked for is still enclosed when you get this scribbly letter from a tired fisherman. See you in my dreams.

Love you, Craig

P.S. I called Barb and Bruce tonight to tell them to pick the frozen salmon, halibut and cod up at the airport. They sounded glad to hear from me and worried about you because of the infrequent mail service.

July, 1977
Port Etches,
Prince William Sound

Dear Dena,

It is the weekend and I am once again taking care of the boat at anchor in Port Etches. Good sunny weather, and I went out to Seal Rocks with the Fish and Wildlife guys that are stationed here. It is a sea lion rookery and really amazing. The sea lions form groups of hundreds and follow the skiff around roaring… the huge Steller sea lion bulls are formidable masses of amazingly graceful flesh! Many dark pups that are still fearless… we put on face mask and snorkel and watched them swim beneath the skiff.

It was a bird survey, of course, and we counted kittiwakes, rock sandpipers, surfbirds, ruddy and black turnstones, wandering tattlers. Visited a rookery of common murres and saw tufted puffins and their burrows. Watched storm petrels flit above the waves.

Greatest of all, we had Dall's porpoise riding our bow and swinging around and under the skiff. It was great leaning over the bow as they threw plumes of water soaking me… they watching me watch them. Such a beautiful example of natural fitness!

I'll go crazy as soon as seining is over and am dying to kayak out into the Sound. There are mountains to climb, whales to watch, fish to catch and I need my partner! We just made a 1000 fish set… that's $240 for one hour's work. Too bad it's not like that all the time. When that big bag of flipping fish is hauled up alongside the boat it really moves the adrenalin! The up-at-4 AM and to–bed-at-midnight is getting a bit wearisome.

A few days later

This letter is getting rambling and strung out just as I am. Last night we almost blew the engine when the water pump belt came off… up almost all night, fishing all day… Thank you for your encouragement and support, and you hit the nail on the head when you talk of our being so occupied with establishing our self. I think I am willing to make a more unified assault on life with you.

To hold each other as the basis of our action while maintaining our individuality is most important.

My parents come up next week, and Pete will be getting someone to replace me for a couple days. Hard to take a day off when you're making an average of $300 a day! The latest word is that seining may last another two or more weeks. Insane.

At least we can spend some time in Cordova to look for a boat, do some berry picking, hunting, etc. until we feel we must head back to school in Fairbanks.

See you soon… I send you my love, be patient, it's not much longer. I am very proud of my research biologist wife.

Love, Craig

August, 1977
Cordova, Alaska

Dear Dena,

We had the first good southeast blow yesterday and accompanying rain. We were traveling from Knight Island to Montague. It was a gas riding the swells, watching for whales. This week we've been fishing the Knight Island/Chenega area, much to my delight and, of course, have been seeing marine mammals like crazy. Found a great cliff for an observation post on Squire Island, and a small anchorage nearby.

Sunday, we ran into a group of nine killer whales actively feeding on salmon. They were so absorbed in feeding they made no reaction to our approach. They were rolling on their backs slapping their tails in obvious ecstasy. One calf was rolling on his mother's back. I could have followed for hours, but we could only stay a few minutes. Yesterday we saw another group of about 75 killer whales, widely spread and traveling.

Have also seen numerous minke whales and over 100 Dall's porpoise. Only one humpback, though, breaching some distance away. It was great getting over on the western side; now we are fishing out on Montague Island. This is the fifth week of the season and we are all getting pretty burned out.

A few days later

Well, my parents have been here and left and the regular seining season has ended. Should be a few emergency openers next week... I hope... as I want to work as much as I can, while I can. It is a real bummer to not be busy every minute... it just gets lonely and I think about you.

I took my parents kayaking and hiking on the glacier and berry picking. They seemed to really enjoy it, but were in Cordova only a few days. They went to Glacier Bay and saw humpback whales and Gustavus.

They feel we should buy land soon, and they were pushing for Gustavus since we could grow things there as well as fish... at times my Dad sounded like he wanted me to become a farmer! They feel the only wise investment is land.

I am looking at boats… a lot for sale and some good deals. I am patiently waiting for you before I do anything… how soon? Lots of plans and possibilities to talk over with you. It's getting so that I feel my hands are tied until we are back together as I want to plan for our lives together, not simply my desires apart from yours. If there is any way you can leave there even a few days early, please do it.

Not much else to say except I love you…

Craig

January, 1978
Kona, Hawaii

Howdy Folks,

And Happy Anniversary! Hope all is well with you and family and Wog dog, oh yes and Ooner cat. We are presently camping in a campground on the Kona coast, trying to adapt our pale northern bodies to this unbelievably intense sunshine, and our tender feet to black lava. What a switch… a land of eternal summer.

Takes a while to really sink in! We find that being toughened to the north does nothing toward preparing one for life in the south. Of course to thoroughly appreciate all that is here, it would only do to stay at least a year. Ah, too bad the north is calling!

This side of the island of Hawaii is the dry side, and in fact can be classified as a desert. A drought has been declared in this area; there's been a notable lack of rain for some time now. On the other side of the island and higher up the mountain slopes there is a great deal more rain and lush forests.

Mostly we've been going snorkeling every day and diving into that incredible world of the coral reefs. We are learning some of the many multi-colored fishes that live in these shallow areas.

This is also the area that the Alaskan humpback whales come to winter, breed and bear young. Yesterday we watched from shore as two breached in unison… what a sight! Today as we were diving, we heard some humpbacks singing underwater nearby. Also saw a group of about a dozen Pacific bottlenose dolphins cruise by.

Bye for now, Dena

March, 1978
Cordova, Alaska

Dear Kirk,

Just to let you know your birthday present will be forthcoming, but lately I've been prevented from doing as much pottery as I've wanted because I've been working so much. Now I'm just going to be life-guarding and teaching at the swimming pool on a part-time basis, so I should have more time for the things I want to do.

As a matter of fact, at this very moment I'm sitting here in my pottery studio waiting for some clay to dry a little so I can work it. I'm pretty well set up here… a wheel borrowed from the school, and an electric kiln downstairs to fire it all.

Today it is snowing, but fairly warm. Spring is just around the corner, and on sunny days, it seems like summertime. We are anxious to set up the kayak and do some trips nearby out in the Sound. We have some friends living out in a cove about 12 miles from town, and we'd like to paddle out and visit them.

Our house on the lake is fixed up really nice and cozy. Wish you could come visit… there are construction jobs opening up, as well as jobs on boats as the fishing season begins. Lots of competition, but with determination, things happen.

Summer plans should begin to crystallize here soon. Craig will find out for sure on his proposal around the end of the month. We're keeping our fingers crossed, because that would mean doing research together on his marine mammal/fishery interaction study.

Besides having jobs and all food paid for the summer, we'd get money for improvements and gas on the boat.

I hear you got a job for the time being… has it ever stopped raining down there? When you're rich again, you really should come on up. We'd like to buy land and build a house either this summer or fall… as soon as possible anyway.

Write and let me know what you're up to. Our address should stay the same for some time to come. Happy birthday.

Love, Dena, Craig and Sol

February, 1979
Cordova, Alaska

Dear Kirk,

Well, I've been so inconsiderate in answering your November letter. There's no grand excuse… I'm just so wrapped up in what I'm doing it puts me out of communication. I hope you were pleased with the set of mugs I made for you and are getting use out of them.

I also hope you are still planning to come up here, and have been saving the money you're making. The only way to go about getting a job in construction or fishing is to come up and get at it. There is work to be had.

We are both pretty wiped out from the work we've been doing (Craig on his thesis, and me teaching pottery) and are in need of a vacation. So we are leaving for Hawaii this weekend. We are planning to spend about three weeks in Hawaii, then spend a week or so in Seattle getting things for our boat, and ordering the materials for our house we're building this fall.

Anyway, our spring and summer plans are not solidified completely as yet, but we will most likely be out fishing or out chasing whales in the Sound in early summer, coming into town occasionally. Then Craig will for sure go seining in mid and late summer.

I am planning to have a group of teen-age kids out on Squire Island to teach them about marine mammal surveys. We will be camping out there for a month, climbing up to the top of a bluff that overlooks a huge part of western Prince William Sound to record the movements of all the marine mammals we see.

This fall Craig and I are planning to go down to Gustavus (where we bought five acres of land) and begin building our house. This is where you definitely come in. It is a neat place, and we could sure use your help. You could work in Cordova this summer, then come down and build our house with us this fall. Or if you have a good job now, wait to come up until later on in the summer. What do you think?

I sure can't guarantee your social life, and sometimes there's too much rain, but it sure would be a new experience for you, and you've just got to get out of California for a while. Your friend is welcome. Let me know.

Love, Dena

May, 1979
Gustavus, Alaska

Dear Kirk,

I'm sending you this list of stuff you should have when you come up that might be useful… you probably have thought of most of it already, and it is by no means complete. If you don't have some of it (like raingear) it would be cheaper to buy it there before coming.

Craig and I are in Gustavus now, clearing the land where the house will be and building a shed. It's really nice here now, sunny and green. This fall we will all be staying in tents on our land, so if you and Charlie could bring up a tent that would be temporarily livable for the two of you, that would be great. When in Cordova, though, you can stay in our house. Craig is leaving tomorrow to head back to Cordova to fish and I will be staying on here another week in hopes that the barge with all our house materials arrives.

If you come to Cordova by about mid-June, you and Charlie can take turns going out gillnetting with Craig in the Sound and getting paid a percentage of what fish are caught. There is some construction going on in town, too.

During the month of July, I am going to be across the Sound near Whale Bay with a group of 17 to 23 year olds, teaching them how to gather scientific information in the field. In this case, it will be information about humpback whales primarily. So I won't be seeing you much at all then, but you will probably be fishing or working, too.

Get in touch and let me know when you arrive. Can't wait!

Love, Dena

April, 1980
Cordova, Alaska

Dear Dena,

Wanted to let you know I have arrived safely. There is a bit of tension here as no one has made any money and everyone is typically broke. Pete has gained about 40 pounds and quit smoking. He is talking about going to Bristol Bay for kelping there after this ends here.

So I hope kelping goes well. Hard to know what the future may bring but I am glad you don't have to be partner to my worry and frustrations now. I have got to deal with my heavy headedness but don't know quite how. I haven't felt so insecure and worried in a long time. Don't you worry, it's not your fault and just something I have to deal with. Hang in there and enjoy yourself in Gustavus.

I have been getting telegrams like crazy from ADFG offices all over S.E. Alaska with job offers. I am almost ready to grab one just to feel more "secure" and be closer to home. (Cordova definitely doesn't feel like home anymore... weird). All the Fish and Game job offers conflict with seine season so far. We shall see. It would be a month and a half in the bush for me. Can we handle that? I will call before I do anything as an ADFG job would probably mean not seeing you for some time. It might allow me to sit on top of a mountain for a bit, though.

Got the boat in the water, running great, and now my diver has cancelled out on me! Kelping will not begin for another several days, so I have a little time. Got to stay cool and figure it out, find another diver. If I do this again it will be me diving and you sorting. Divers are just too much, too crazy.

Otherwise, life progresses. Got a call from USFWS this morning and they want us to continue marine mammal work in the southwestern Sound. They are going to try to find some funding for us for after seine season. Sounds good to me and I will fill you in on details as they develop.

Went out to Jacksons on Sunday and had a hot tub and a great time. Beautiful spot they've got on the lake. Everyone here asks about you constantly... even Brook.

Don't worry about money but please try to be conservative. Will write again when all is a bit more together. It is nice to know

I have a home to return to when this craziness is over. Take care, sweetie.

    Love, Craig

April, 1980
Port Fidalgo,
Prince William Sound

Dear Dena,

A lot of water has passed under the bridge since I last wrote. I spent days calling all over and walking the docks and waiting at the airport looking for another diver. Most all the divers were already set up. So I had to get out of town and went with Jack Shaw on the *Islander* to run jitney and seine up some herring for the pounds that Pete and crew built.

ADFG changed the rules and made it nearly impossible to seine, and we could not get as many fish as we needed. Still, we did prove that the pounding technique is feasible. I missed a call from a diver and the season is now opening for wild kelp harvest. Such is life. Looks like I will be going around and picking up kelp for the next few days and the spawn has not been too good. I have been enjoying myself and have gotten a little more seining experience, but am making bare wages. Things will improve.

The weather has been godawful... snowed and blew for the last couple days. It's cold! Jack Shaw and I are headed into town with a load of kelp from the ponds. Many minke whales and scoters. Have been watching the herring spawning in the early mornings. The whole scene is really incredible... all the birds and harbor seals so fat and satiated they can barely dive. Herring moving and spawning like clouds driven before the wind. When I am out like this money doesn't seem too important... not till I get to town and see the prices!!

Salmon seining should be a lot of fun if the money pressure is not too great. Jack has been helping me get mentally ready for seining (he was running the *Islander* and I ran the jitney). His approach is much different than Pete's and a welcome change. He approaches everything slowly and methodically.

Take care of the garden and I hope house-building and ceramics is progressing. It is time I reestablished some goals and really tried to direct my existence or I may soon end up in the limbo type of existence that engulfs so many people. Oh well...

Next letter will be more positive, I promise. I love and miss you but am just as glad you are not in the quagmire here. I want to relate to you about positive and good things when next I see you.

I feel bad that I haven't been around to help you through what was no doubt a tough experience. I hope losing the pregnancy has not upset you too much. I hope you are feeling better and that you will be happy. It will probably all be easier next time. We still have lots of time for a family, and hopefully I will be more prepared mentally. Babies will come soon enough. I was just getting used to the idea of becoming a father. Don't be lonely, sweetie.

      Love you,
      Craig

May, 1980
Cordova, Alaska

Dear Dena,

 The first shore birds are arriving at Hartney Bay among the blowing snow and rain. Westerns and dunlins in small flocks... not quite a thousand yet. A black turnstone or two and the call of a dowitcher.
 Kelping was closed after three days due to lack of spawn. Only a few people did well. Things will work out... I think I am starting to relax a bit. We may be close to broke but have many things going for us. All will work out.
 Pete and I seem to be communicating a bit better now... I get the feeling he has developed more understanding for my situation. He is definitely growing as a person. Today he left for Bristol Bay to take delivery of his new boat and was joking and friendly. He was very concerned about you. I look forward to seining his boat... the *Starling* is fun to run and should work well. Start getting yourself psyched up because it will be work like you won't believe. (It shocked me that first year). Should be a good time.
 When I am out in the Sound I feel great... I had forgotten how much I loved it. Don't know if I can ever let go of Prince William Sound. I will probably move onto the *Starling* in a few days and that will be our home away from home. How does the garden go? Hope Sol is doing all right and that you are maintaining a positive attitude. I miss you much and will be glad when we are back together. I guess you should come up as soon as your parents leave.
 I have been traveling rapidly as of late. In Anchorage I met with people at USFWS about whale work. Right now I am writing a "mini-proposal" to get a couple thousand dollars for surveys this fall. Went on to Fairbanks, fixed up the thesis and had it final typed all in a day and a half and then started it circulating. Had a great time on a birding field trip that was headed for Cordova. Saw a tremendous number of birds and had a great sunny ferry ride from Valdez to Cordova, saw many minke whales and a couple of humpbacks.
 What you say is quite true... it is time to narrow down and

concentrate. Choosing a viable occupation that does not conflict with the rest of our lives and can satisfy both my mental and physical needs. Does it exist? It is time to get focused although my current situation seems to make this difficult. I don't think that separation as such is the answer, but certainly time alone is necessary to sort out priorities. It seems we must together make mutual decisions, or neither of us will be satisfied.

I haven't had the chance to sit on my mountain yet, but I have spent the last five days storm bound on the *Tarka II* behind Wingham Island. We made a pull of Bill's tanner crab pots as the weather deteriorated. Pulling the 120-pound pots requires about 14-16 hours of endless quick work on deck, with a six foot swell and 30 mph winds. Makes Dungeness crab fishing look like a picnic. We did manage to get out and dig a slug of razor clams, and many of them are upstairs in the freezer for you.

>I love you so take care and make progress,
>Craig

September, 1980
Gustavus, Alaska

Dear Kirk,

You were right, we were surprised when we got here. It really makes a difference having that side of the house finished. The porch is just what we had in mind. It all looks very professional… very good job! Also got car parts (thanks for sending them) and installed them before the torrential rain began yesterday. (It seems to be bright sun or torrential rain lately).

Also managed to install the new heat stove in the living room before the rain started. It was a bit of a job because the path of the pipe went right through a rafter, so had to build headers and work in the tight space between roof and ceiling. It's in now and looks good, although we need something to cover the elliptical space between the pipe and the ceiling.

The neighbors shot a bear (Flo, alias "deadeye," nailed it) and gave it to us, so we cleaned, skinned, butchered and canned it and also had a big bear-stew party.

Don't know how much I'll get done on the house this fall since I have a ton of paperwork to do, including a paper for a conference and a USFWS contract paper. So much remains to be done!

We aren't rich no more as I bought a gillnet permit and bowpicker (Yep, a real live ugly bowpicker). So now I owe about $20,000. I do include money for the parts and a little for your efforts. (This money goes to school expense only!). Hope you enjoyed Gustavus and school is going ok.

Craig

March, 1981
Gustavus, Alaska

Dear Kirk,

Wanted to say Happy Birthday and good cheer and hope you had a good time and I was thinking about you and can't remember how old you are. Getting old like the rest of us now, aren't you? Don't worry, there really is life after thirty!

Spring seems to be finding its way to Gustavus… we've had a few outrageous sunny days which reminds us of all the work there is to do outside, of course. More trees to cut down and haul away, more garden to dig up, seeds to order, etc. etc. I think we're actually going to start putting up poles for the kiln shed so I can get to building the kiln this summer.

Craig finished the cabinets in the kitchen and, with the top already tiled, it looks great. The tub and sink are in with drains in the bathroom, and I laid tiles around the sink. Now I just have to make and fire the tiles for around the tub.

Craig is leaving to go kelping near Cordova in a couple weeks while I stay here to teach a tile-making class and get the garden going. I'll be going up to Cordova for pink salmon seining again sometime in June. We're playing it all by ear, as usual. I enjoy my freedom here and the peace and quiet of Life with the Wog.

I realize I'm getting very spoiled living among the luxuries of constant fresh air and open space. The recent snows have made everything very beautiful and winter-like again. Craig and I are forming a non-profit research corporation called North Gulf Oceanic Society. All our marine research will be done under that name now.

Thanks so much for sending the painting you did of the house… it is beautiful and is up on the kitchen wall now. And the tape is excellent… we really enjoy it.

What are your plans? Anything solid yet? Keep in touch.

Love, Dena

June, 1981
Cordova, Alaska

Dear Folks,

We're out on the boat fishing now… it opened really early this year. It's a bit scanty, but we're doing fairly well. This year is supposed to be the biggest yet for salmon seining in Prince William Sound. Feels great to be out on the water again with our same two crew. Should be a long season, so it's nice we get along.

Kirk and Pam arrived the day we left and we'll see them on weekends until they head for Gustavus. Pam is working as a maid, and Kirk may get on a tender again.

Do you realize that Craig and I have been married for five whole years?? And been together for eight years… almost a decade!

We got in the four log pillars that will be the supports for my kiln shed in Gustavus. It will be a wood-fueled kiln that I'll be building when we get back there this fall. I'm collecting dry lumber scraps to burn in the kiln, and it should help immensely in getting up to temperature. When I am in Gustavus, pottery rules my life!

The garden was up and doing well by the time I left to come fishing for pink salmon again. Getting into the steady pace of life with three guys on a boat. I do most of the cooking, which is fine and gets me out of having to sling dead fish to the tender that buys them at the end of the day. Fun!

Craig is a good captain, and is definitely getting seining figured out. I am learning to run the jitney (small skiff that tows the seine usually toward the beach, then back to the boat to purse up the net and trap the fish). So there is still a lot for me to learn, which keeps it interesting.

Happy Father's Day! For now… much love to you,

Dena

September, 1981
Gustavus, Alaska

Dear Kirk,

We were very impressed by your handiwork and am very glad that I don't have to do that end wall this fall. Much else to do.

The garden looks real good, the peas really did it. You should have eaten more lettuce.

Yes, the season was a good one but many expenses. By the time I am finished buying new engines, etc. we will be far from rich.

Start keeping your eyes open for a Datsun truck. We will want to buy one as soon as we get to California in early November.

Thank you again for all your labors… check is enclosed.

Craig

After talking to you on the phone yesterday, I realized we hadn't sent this letter and check which you were probably wondering about. I was supposed to add to the letter Craig started and send it on. Sorry… things have been pretty squirrelly around here.

We will be at the Haskell family Thanksgiving gathering at Barb's for sure. And Craig's brother Roger is getting married sometime during our California visit.

Hope I got across on the phone how much we like what you did on the house. You sure saved us a lot of time and trouble by doing the end wall siding… big job! And the railing upstairs is definitely first class.

Love, Dena

April, 1982
Gustavus, Alaska

Dear Lee,

Wanting to wish a happy birthday to you, and hoping this finds you feeling younger than your age!

It's very peaceful here now… Craig has left for Cordova, so Sol and I are awaiting spring together. Still a couple feet of snow, but the sun keeps pouring down in tropical proportions which helps make the transition from southern to northern hemisphere a great deal easier.

Been doing lots of skiing… I went snow camping one night with Sol out on the flats on the other side of the Good River… brr! Mostly we've been hauling in by sled everything we got on our trip. To haul in furniture and big things like that, we use a car hood that is turned over and becomes a sled. Tell Mama and Daddy the treadle sewing machine arrived in perfect shape… only fell over once but no damage done.

I put up a rod in the downstairs bedroom to create a closet, so now for the first time in three years my dresses and blouses are hanging on hangers instead of being folded up in boxes and dresser!

Now I'm going to begin on the bathroom. I just got the wallpaper, and that will make a big difference, plus painting around the tub where I'll be putting the tiles I'm making. We even have a shower curtain we bought ages ago. Hopefully I can make it look enough like a bathroom so that my plumber will be inspired to put hot running water in it.

We will be fishing in the Sound until sometime in September, then hope to run a seine boat down across the Gulf to Gustavus with our first skiff, the *Goldeneye*, on its deck. Do you want to drive our truck (and Sol) from Cordova to Juneau? That involves taking it on the ferry to Valdez, driving the Alaska highway through Canada to Haines, then taking the ferry to Juneau. From there you could fly to Gustavus.

All this is in the embryonic planning stages and dependent on various factors that will unfold as the summer fishing season unfolds. Sound vague and crazy enough?

So, if you can make plans from there, let me know. We'll be in touch.

Love, Dena

May, 1982
Cordova, Alaska

Dear Folks and all,

    We are back in town after the first fishing period. During the 36-hour opener we caught 2 trees and about 800 red salmon and a few kings. We are getting a lot less per pound for them this year... only a dollar instead of $1.50 last year. Humpies may only bring 15 cents a pound during seine season. Oh well, gotta work for a living this year... twice as hard for half as much. Such is the sad tune of us poor fishermen!

    Gillnetting out of a bowpicker is pretty deluxe, though. We've done a lot of work on making the boat more efficient and comfortable. It's amazing what a little paint, linoleum and wallpaper (just a bit!) can do for a boat. At least there promises to be lots of fish... they were hitting the net in schools, sometimes ten at a time coming into the boat all wound up in the net together. Our fingers were swollen and sore from picking them out! The weather wasn't too bad... always a wind, though.

    I'm flying down to Gustavus next Sunday, the 30th. I'll be there about a week putting in the garden... flying back up here on June 8. I got someone taking care of Sol while we're out fishing and when I'm in Gustavus. The people live in the cabin where I used to work in the studio and fire pots in the wood-fired kiln (the one I disassembled and took to Gustavus). So anyway, Sol is plenty at home there since spending so much time there with me. He seems a bit slower these days, but still wants to run a lot and is the same personality-wise.

    We are still living at the APA Cannery (lots of the other fishermen stay here, too... a few young couples like us). Tonight we're going to dinner at the Addingtons' and show them the slides of our trip to Fiji, Australia and New Zealand.

    Just before leaving Gustavus, I planted two apple trees in the yard. Just barely leafing out with leaves and scented white blossoms. Can't wait to get back and see what bulbs came up in the garden.

    You can call at Pete's anytime to get hold of us. We'll always get the message.

    Love, Dena

March, 1983
Gustavus, Alaska

Dear Kirk,

I guess I've been a bit flakey about my communications, but usually you don't win any prizes in that area yourself, so you can understand.

First of all... we really did like the towel holder you sent for Christmas. We sent it on up to Cordova for the new place there. Craig is now doing the finishing touches on the upstairs apartment, and I'm planning on going up just after the first of April to do the final finishing touches. So I'll see it for the first time in a couple weeks.

At the moment, I am glazing and firing the pots and tiles I've been making for the show I'm having in Cordova later this summer, after the baby is born. Yes, it does look to be a relatively insane year for us, but that's no different than usual. My big belly is due to hatch in late June (peak week of fishing).

Craig won't be seining the *Starling* this year; he's worked another deal with a guy that doesn't want to fish anymore. Three other guys will be crew who already have experience. Craig is skipper, of course.

I'm just playing everything by ear from now on. I'll keep you posted.

Love, Dena

July, 1983
Cordova, Alaska

To the Haskell Family:

Eve Steller Matkin
has joined us

July 8, 1983
10:13 AM
8 lbs. 5 oz.

Friday's child is loving and giving

Craig and Dena Matkin

CHAPTER 5: Glacier Bay, Gustavus and Eve wisdom

November, 1983
Gustavus, Alaska

Dear Kirk and Pam,

I want to thank you for your cute little gift to Eve. The sweater will keep her nice and toasty through many a chilly Alaskan winter.

Eve and I are leaving for Colorado on Saturday. Sounds like winter is arriving there, too. I'm planning on spending time near Aspen, skiing and doing pottery.

Don't feel bad about Craig's and my divorce. In many ways the marriage was over years ago, and I have already spent enough time mourning its passage. Now it's just a matter of formalities and I already feel so much better about myself.

And I have Eve, who gives me a great deal of strength and purpose. Sometimes I actually feel exhilarated, knowing the future is wide open for me.

Hope things go well for you two. Work hard and have fun.

Love, Dena

June, 1985
Gustavus, Alaska

Dear Kirk,

Hi... actually feeling fairly wonderful about being in Gustavus at the moment. Sun! lots of flowers coming along in the garden, and Eve able to get out and enjoy it all, too. Ahh... the easy life as I remember it.

Craig and I are finalizing the divorce at last. He has agreed to give me sole custody of Eve, so that will all be settled soon, after we get the three-months visitation figured out. It's close.

I will definitely be getting electricity in the next couple months. It will make building the bay window easier when you come up in August. Could you bring up the right joist hangers when you come?

As far as the kayak trip goes, there is a plane that can take us out to the outer coast, and we would pay half of a charter. Coming back, maybe we could catch a ride on a fishing boat or something. Well, there's a little time to figure it out.

Been getting out in Glacier Bay with the Park whale biologist a few times. Once we took Eve, and we got close to humpbacks. So I finally got the needed inspiration to finish the humpback design. Also finished my spy-hopping orca whale design for the annual Gustavus t-shirt. I've been taking Eve kayaking in the Klepper, which she enjoys.

My strength and self-confidence are returning.

Hope things are tolerable down there and your camping trip was fun.

Call before you leave.

Love, Dena

February 14, 1993
Gustavus, Alaska

For Eve:

Beautiful dancer, faithful friend,
Clever writer, swimmer,
Artist to the end.

The light of my life, my reason to be,
The answer to my prayers,
You make my heart free.

Good, kind and sweet, you teach lessons of love.
My daughter, my treat,
Are you really an angel sent from above?

Happy Valentine's Day
Love forever, Dena Mom

June, 1995
Homer, Alaska

Dear Mom, (Dena)

How are you doing in Gustavus? I am having lots of fun. Strawberry's colt is so cute. We also got some baby ducks and they are so cute. My duck follows me around everywhere and when I sit he jumps on my lap. I really love baby ducks even better than colts.

If I don't tell you this before I call you then I need my helmet for riding.

I miss you. I am starting to get really homesick. I wish I could see you so bad. Well I can't find the cards that I got for Easter. I don't mind if I don't find them because I like making cards for you. I got new crayons 64 new crayons.

I also made something beautiful for you.

Well I've got to go to bed.

bye
love always,
Eve

P.S. Please call me when you get this.
I miss you

Fall, 1995
Gustavus, Alaska

POEMS
By Eve Matkin
(Age 12)

Metaphors

War is a mist of anger
The moon is a light that is not there
Heaven is a rose without thorns
Hate is a weed growing in a flower garden
Shoes are the end of you and the beginning of the world

Tears

Tears are pain of the heart
Falling liquid from the eyes reasons not known
Wet but dry in the heart
Happiness not able to be found

Snow

Love is snow
Pure as a crystal taken from the earth
Delicate and sweet like a cold spring breeze
Fluffy as two red lips
Cold as a broken heart wetted by tears

Thirteen

Giggles like a gull
Rebellious as a cow
Unlucky as a bug are your parents at your whim
You want to be free as the wind
But there are some that love always their parents

January, 1996
Gustavus, Alaska

PERSUASIVE ESSAY ABOUT GUSTAVUS
By Eve Matkin (Age 12)

I have lived in Gustavus all my life. I have traveled and seen other parts of the world. I know what it's like. So I always come back to Gustavus and I am glad it is my home and I think it is a good place to live.

Gustavus is not a big city; I don't think a big city would be a very nice place to live. That is just what I think because I have lived in a little town. Most cities have 10 stores, 6 gas stations and 5 airports. Well I guess big cities need all that stuff because they have so many people. Gustavus doesn't have that many people so we don't need that much of everything. The only thing I think that we really need here is a swimming pool and a movie theater.

Gustavus is very in touch with nature. I mean I can walk out my door and not see a house or a person and I can be surrounded by nature. I can see bears in my front yard and I have had ravens steal my Easter eggs.

Glacier Bay National Park is very nice, too. I have seen whales from the dock and I have seen grouse and moose on the road. One time I even saw a family of porcupines on the road. There are squirrels everywhere, chattering and collecting pine cones and mushrooms.

This is what I saw one Halloween night. I had finished trick-or-treating, and my mom and I decided to go to the beach to eat and look at my candy. Just as we got to the beach, northern lights of many colors began dancing across the sky. It was so beautiful the way they filled the entire sky for about a half an hour.

Transportation isn't a problem in the summer. There are boats and airplanes can fly. In the winter the boats go to tropical hot places and the airplanes have a hard time flying but they do get out sometimes. So if you live here you have to like snow, ice and not mind dressing warmly. Or at least you have to not mind it that much.

Well now I have told you a little bit about Gustavus in the summer and winter. Which means you have to take the good with the bad.

May, 1996
Gustavus, Alaska

A CRAZY EASTER
By Eve Matkin
(Age 12)

Once upon a Easter, me and my mom were sleeping and my mom woke up and looked out the window. She saw a raven flying in the air with a pink thing in his mouth.

Then she remembered it was Easter and knew it was an Easter egg. So she ran outside and tried to scare away all the ravens that tried to get my Easter eggs. After I woke up, I went outside to find my Easter eggs, then I went inside to count them, and two were missing.

About a year later we were walking through the woods and we stumbled upon one of my Easter eggs. It was hidden under a fallen log. We could hardly believe our eyes.

So from now on, my mom has to wake up really early so she can scare away the ravens.

February 14, 1997
Gustavus, Alaska

Eve:

Two-ton butterfly,
shimmering cocoon,
you are as lovely
as an eclipse
of the moon.

Mom

November, 1997
Homer, Alaska

Dear Dena,

I can't tell you how healing it was to see you in Sitka. Certainly it is not as if we have resolved all our issues, but I felt an emotional honesty and openness with you that I have not been able to manifest before. Thanks for being willing to let down some of the barriers we have had. I don't think I realized how important it is to have some resolution and completion with you. It is good to feel you as a friend again.

I was very impressed at how much stronger an individual you are now than when you were with me. I realize my role in not really aiding you in your development. I am glad that you have found such positive outlets for your energy. It was great to hear you talk about the satisfactions of your Park Naturalist job… and also of the frustrations. Good for you for maintaining and developing what you have.

And of course it is great to feel the sharing of Eve as a mutual joy and partnership rather than a "my way" and "your way" situation. As you and I have dropped the hostility over the past few years, my relationship with Eve has improved tremendously.

There are many lessons in life, some seem to take at least a lifetime to learn. It is frightening and exhilarating at the same time.

I hope we continue our friendship with as much mutual understanding as possible.

With affection, Craig

November, 1997
Gustavus, Alaska

Poem by Dena Matkin

Eve Steller
Child of El Nino,
your time to be born.
Rain-healed tears.
A family
baptized in waves of forgiveness.
Bubbling smooth foam
dispersing huge forces,
reversing momentum,
uniting three souls
in momentary song.
Friends
Bound for movin' on.
In this winter season,
searching for
a time for every purpose
under heaven,
we found a time
for peace.

January, 1998
Gustavus, Alaska

By Eve Matkin (Age 14):

FOLK BALLAD

A lady of the whales was she
To learn of ways they were
She wished to know the secrets
The secrets of the past

Stout was she to face such gods
The possessors of the sea
She knew there are things they not possess
That's humans and their vanity

MY GRANDMA

My grandma is an extraordinary person. She lives in suburbia but she doesn't waste a thing or do a single thing that's bad for the earth. She also is really good at exercising and takes very good care of her body.

She thinks solar energy is one of the best things in the world. She cooks with it, heats her water with it and she tries to get other people to use it. When she visits, she almost always gets the solar cooker out and bakes a pie or something in it. She is always donating to environmental and health organizations. My grandma has plenty of money but she tries not to use a lot of energy, she tries not to buy very much, and is always finding new ways to use less.

One thing that she is really crazy about that I used to hate is vinegar. I remember her washing my face and hands with it and how disgusting the smell was to me. My grandma uses it for washing her hair, windows and tons of other things. One of the reasons she likes it so much is because it is a natural disinfectant and if it's natural, she likes it. Now I don't mind the smell of vinegar so much, probably because she doesn't wash me with it anymore, and because it reminds me of her.

Grandma is so disciplined when it comes to exercising. Every day she does yoga and walks on her treadmill. Twice a week she goes swimming and there are many other things that she does to stay in good health. She has a strict schedule. She wakes up at the same time every day, has breakfast, lunch and dinner at the same time and does everything the same each week.

I think this is pretty amazing for a 77 year old woman, but that's probably why she'll live so long. I love Grandma Doris because she has taught me consistency, discipline and the importance of taking care of the earth and family.

October, 1998
Gustavus, Alaska

ORCA P. MATKIN
By Eve Matkin
(Age 15)

It was a cold October afternoon when I got my dog Orca. We were getting ready to go do some errands, and I went outside to wait. As I neared our old car I saw a big bag of dog food. At that moment I thought nothing of it. Then when we got in the car I asked my mom what it was for, and she said that we had gotten it for a friend of ours. So I just shrugged it off and totally forgot about it.

As we were driving down the road we met up with Jon Lesh. We stopped and my mom said something to him but I couldn't understand what they were saying. We turned around and went back to our house. I was a little exasperated because I had been trying to get my mom out the door all day. I reluctantly agreed to go back, but I made her promise that we wouldn't take a long time.

When we drove up, Jon was parked in the driveway. I hopped out. Jon went to the back of his truck and opened it. Right when I saw the kennel I knew exactly what was going on. I screamed for joy and ran to the two most adorable black puppies I had ever seen. We let them out and they ran around like they had never been outside before. They looked so happy and playful, it just made me want to laugh.

I picked one up and he licked my face and squirmed to get free so he could go play with his brother. They were almost impossible to tell apart except that one of them was smaller than the other. Jon wanted the smaller one, so we took the other. I thanked him and told him how grateful I was.

We took a little Puppy Chow in the truck with us, which was a mistake from the beginning. Orca ate a little, but he was so nervous in the truck that he didn't feel like eating. Almost the whole drive he was whining. Finally, as we neared the dump he stopped and fell asleep on my lap. My mom got out of the truck to talk to someone and left the door open. Then the puppy woke up and started making these weird sounds. I yelled at my mom and she whirled around and grabbed Orca by the scruff of the neck and yanked him out of the truck. He threw up right as my mom got him out of the truck. He walked around and then he was fine.

    I have had many more experiences with Orca Pup that I will always remember, but this is my first memory of Orca. He changed my life so much and I don't know how I ever lived without him. When I'm only gone from him for a day I miss him so much.

    You never know how happy your life can be until you get a dog.

December, 1998
Gustavus, Alaska

STORIES
By Eve Matkin (Age 15)

Metaphors

thrown drowning
in a sharp sea
rolling tumbling gashes
torn from me
finally torture is over
I am drying my colors
fading
grasped by a gentle hand
dents caressed

Kayaking

One time when I was very young I went on a kayak trip with my mom and one of her friends. We were going up this river and there were fish jumping everywhere. I had just been talking to my mom about how scary it would be if a fish jumped in our boat. Just then there was a big splash right next to the kayak and a huge salmon fell into my lap.

The way it moved and felt made me realize how strong it was. Its scales were the most beautiful silver and they gave me an urge to feel it. But it was like reaching out to touch moon beams; you just can't quite reach them. It was also extremely heavy and all I wanted was for it to be off me.

I was screaming and flipping out and my mom was flailing at it, trying to get it off. Finally it leaped back out into the water. I looked down and there were scales everywhere. I thought of this because kayaking is one of my favorite outdoor things to do and this is one of the most funny things that's ever happened to me while I was kayaking. I have many other memories that I think of as I write about this, though.

January 23, 1999
Gustavus, Alaska

Dear Eve,

    A while ago, your mom showed me some of your recent writing. It was so beautiful that I simply had to take a moment to tell you how much I enjoyed it, and how proud I am of the lovely young lady you are becoming.
    Loveliness starts from inside. It grows if a person accepts opportunities to love, stays open to the perception and expression of beauty, and hones the skills that nature has given us. You are doing all these things very well, Eve.
    People of my generation need to stop our busy lives once in a while and just say "thank you" to the young people of our community. You are our future, and the source of much of our pride in being Gustavians.
    I want to give you this spoon, Eve. It is made of SE Alaskan yellow cedar and has a carving of a willow on it: your namesake plant (did you know that the word for "willow" in Russian is "eva"?).

    Respectfully,

    Greg Streveler

February 14, 1999
Gustavus, Alaska

Eve:

My teen,
my queen,
oh, how you preen!
You're still the best,
even when I
want to scream.

Night-skiing with
the Moonchild fulfills
more of my dreams.

I love you,
my sweet.
You're a beautiful treat!

Mom

Fall, 1999
Gustavus, Alaska

HOMER
By Eve Matkin
(Age 16)

Homer has changed immensely since my mom and dad lived there in 1974. They lived in a little log cabin that you couldn't drive to. The only way you could get to it was a small dirt road that led to a trail. Now all the major roads are paved. Only the small roads and driveways are unpaved.

Our road has changed a lot over the past few years. Our road was first built by my dad and some friends. After that people started more building. Then people started building roads off ours. Now people are constructing houses all along our road.

Homer has grown especially fast compared to other towns. This is partly due to the highway from Anchorage. It makes it more accessible for cars so people can drive there and not have to spend a lot of money on plane flights. Another reason for its expansion is that it has very beautiful scenery and is a nice tourist destination. Furthermore a lot of Anchorage people have summer homes in Homer.

Some of Homer is very lovely and is a good place to raise a family. My neighborhood is very nice and doesn't have too many people. Homer is still developing because part of the economy depends on tourism. The other part depends on oil. Oil has destroyed lots of habitat on the Kenai Peninsula. In spite of this I love visiting Homer but Gustavus is the place I call home!

December, 2000
Homer, Alaska

PERSONAL ESSAY
By Eve Matkin
(Age 17)

  I grew up in Gustavus, Alaska, a town of less than four hundred people. Gustavus is surrounded by water on three sides and has mountains on the fourth. Last year I decided to go live in Homer, Alaska for my last two years of high school. Homer is more accessible, has more than ten times the population and more characteristics of a city.
  Every summer I traveled to Prince William Sound with my dad, who is a killer whale biologist. Year round, I would go out with my mom to study the same killer whales when they came to Glacier Bay.
  I have grown up surrounded by the most beautiful and wild regions of Alaska. Ever since I can remember I've watched humpback whales bubble-net feeding, killer whales devouring harbor seals, Dall's porpoise riding the bow of our boat and bears contentedly picking berries. Some people would think I take these things for granted, but every time I go out on the water with my parents it makes me appreciate my life, family and Alaska even more.
  When I was a little girl, I remember going to Prince William Sound and being surrounded by killer whales. I could look in any direction and see dozens of whales nearly every day. Then, when I was five years old, the Exxon Valdez tanker spilled eleven million gallons of oil into the Sound. Little did I know that all of this would change. My mom cried sometimes when she saw the carnage on the news or talked to my dad about it. I was so young that I couldn't really understand but I sensed that something horrible had happened.
  A few years later I went back to the Sound and it all seemed different. Many whales had disappeared, and AB pod had lost 14 of 36 individuals. We would have to search hard just to find a few individuals. Even after I saw all the destruction, I still couldn't quite comprehend. I couldn't believe that such a terrible thing

could happen and why my dad couldn't do anything about it.

When I became old enough I realized how important the wilderness and animals of Prince William Sound were to me and decided I could do something to help one of the most beautiful places I have ever been. The Sound is recovering eleven years after the spill and I am certain that I want to be a part of it.

Having these experiences has taught me what is important in my life. I have watched my family and learned so much from the unique example they have set before me. My parents have created their own careers and lives so I know that I can do anything if I want it badly enough. All of these changes have prepared me for the next big transition in my life: leaving home and going to college.

February 14, 2001
Gustavus, Alaska

Eve:

Where do pretty girls come from?

From masses of moonbeams,
Slivers of starlight,
Fields of flowers,
Longing and delight.

You are ripples of laughter,
Waves of a song,
A piece of a mommy
Who loves you so strong.

Love, Mom

CHAPTER 6: Mama story

Mama Story

Essay written sometime in 2000 by Doris Haskell:

Before you see the video (*Whales of Alaska's Inside Passage*) I thought you might like to know of my daughter Dena's background in Alaska, the steps that led to the research she's been doing for the last 15 years. She and her husband Craig met at UC Santa Cruz where they majored in the natural sciences. Upon graduation in 1974 they took off for Homer, Alaska, to work at a seasonal job in a crab cannery. Up a muddy road above town in hills covered with blueberries and fireweed was an abandoned one-room log cabin by a little spring. This was their fairly comfortable headquarters for two years. In summer their vegetable garden flourished and in winter they skied and gathered, cut and stacked all their firewood.

After a year in Alaska, residency requirements were met to gain employment with Alaska Department of Fish and Game. The job was counting salmon at a fish weir on a remote island in Cook Inlet. Food was flown in bi-weekly or even less frequently. Beavers were very busy at the stream and decided it should not be running but needed to be dammed up, which they did each night. Every day Dena and Craig were kept busy opening the stream for the salmon to pass through.

That fall, upon returning to the Homer log cabin, a disaster met them: according to eyewitnesses, a black bear and her two cubs broke in and had a field day. The bears were observed lolling on the bed, licking clean every bit of food and generally destroying everything.

The spring of 1976 Dena and Craig returned to California to be married. They asked their favorite professor, cetologist and natural history instructor to perform the ceremony. He said he couldn't do that, but they convinced him it was possible to obtain one of those funny little licenses, which were legal. So on a beautiful day in April at Professor Ken Norris' home in the Santa Cruz mountains, a long procession of family, friends and former fellow students wound their way to a hilltop for a truly lovely, unique ceremony.

Back in Alaska that summer the next job was salmon tracking on the Eshamy River in Prince William Sound. This time instead of beavers there were black bears who claimed the salmon run. Dena and Craig tried to be courteous and not be too pushy, but after a while had to say, "OK, bears, now it's our turn!"

Fall 1976, Craig decided to obtain his Master's degree in zoology at the University of Alaska in Fairbanks. They moved to another log cabin outside of town. In February 1977 Dena tearfully called to tell me the cabin had burned to the ground during their absence on campus. A wood stove was left burning low to keep the place a little warm for their return. The propane tank then exploded. People on the scene said it was hard to keep their Irish setter dog from rushing into the fire. He apparently thought they were in there.

Research for the Master's thesis meant a move to Cordova to investigate harbor seal and sea lion predation on salmon gillnets. When I visited them there Dena and I went down to the harbor and she questioned commercial fishermen on their experiences with marine mammal encounters. They were eager to tell her all about it. This information was necessary to obtain, and in the long run benefited the fishermen because Craig recommended a device to discourage the seals.

One day I was walking alone along the shore and was awed by the peaceful magnificence of the view, especially the crystal clarity of the water, as clear as our 9,000 foot Sierra lakes, and the snow-capped mountains to the northwest. When my son Kirk went to Cordova to earn summer money by commercial fishing, I commissioned him to get me a photo of those mountains from the shoreline at Cordova. So now I have a "before the spill" picture of Prince William Sound.

Back to Dena and Craig's story. In 1979, deeper roots were established in Alaska by ownership of land. Gustavus, now population about 400, is 30 minutes flying time from Juneau. Friends from Santa Cruz had already built a log home there. A 5-acre piece of forest off a dirt road was purchased and building started in August.

Kirk arrived a couple of weeks before Dena and Craig to help build. For all comforts and conveniences Kirk had a wooden platform to pitch his tent and a shed for supplies close by. It rained most of that month. All building supplies were carried from the road by hand or on a small cart through a narrow path between the trees for about ¼ mile.

It is really an attractive home with four rooms downstairs and a large open upper story. Dena built the outhouse herself, a pretty and sturdy one facing a little meadow with woods beyond, and no door. Now there's complete indoor plumbing.

Daughter Eve was born in 1983. Shortly after, Dena and Craig split up. Craig returned to Homer to continue commercial fishing and whale research. Dena is a Naturalist and also pursues her own orca research in her boat. Eve has always spent a couple of months each year with Craig and has developed a strong affectionate relationship with both her parents. Her life has been full of Alaskan adventures. She has spent weeks on fishing seiners, rafted down the Copper River, skied from her front doorstep, and as a tiny child she went on a kayak trip with Dena, Del and me.

Dena explains that she and Craig have two things in common: Eve and their research. The bitterness of the separation is gone and they cooperate on child rearing and whale research. Craig knows the same individual orcas in Prince William Sound that Dena meets in Glacier Bay, and they have co-authored (with others) a catalogue of the killer whales of southern Alaska.

PART TWO: PHOTOS, DRAWINGS AND STORIES

Above: Craig, Eve, Sol, and Dena Matkin in Gustavus in 1983. Photo by Craig Matkin

Below: T86A Eider, with her calf T86A3 Tyndall and T40 (T2). Photo by Dena Matkin

Above: Craig, Eve, and Dena Matkin at Eve's wedding in Homer. Photo by Linda Smogor

Below: T85 Eve and her family in Glacier Bay in 2011. Photo by Dena Matkin

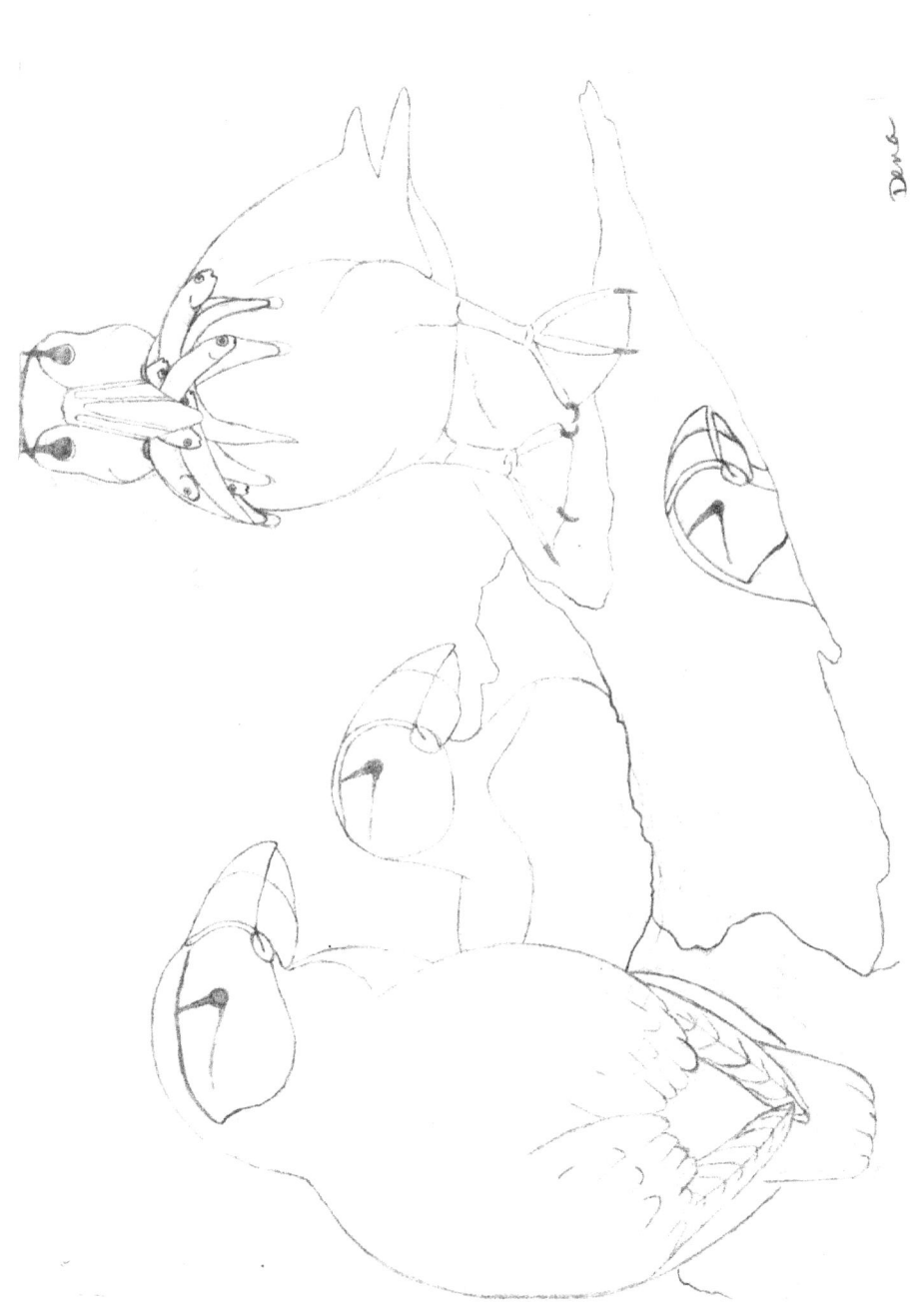

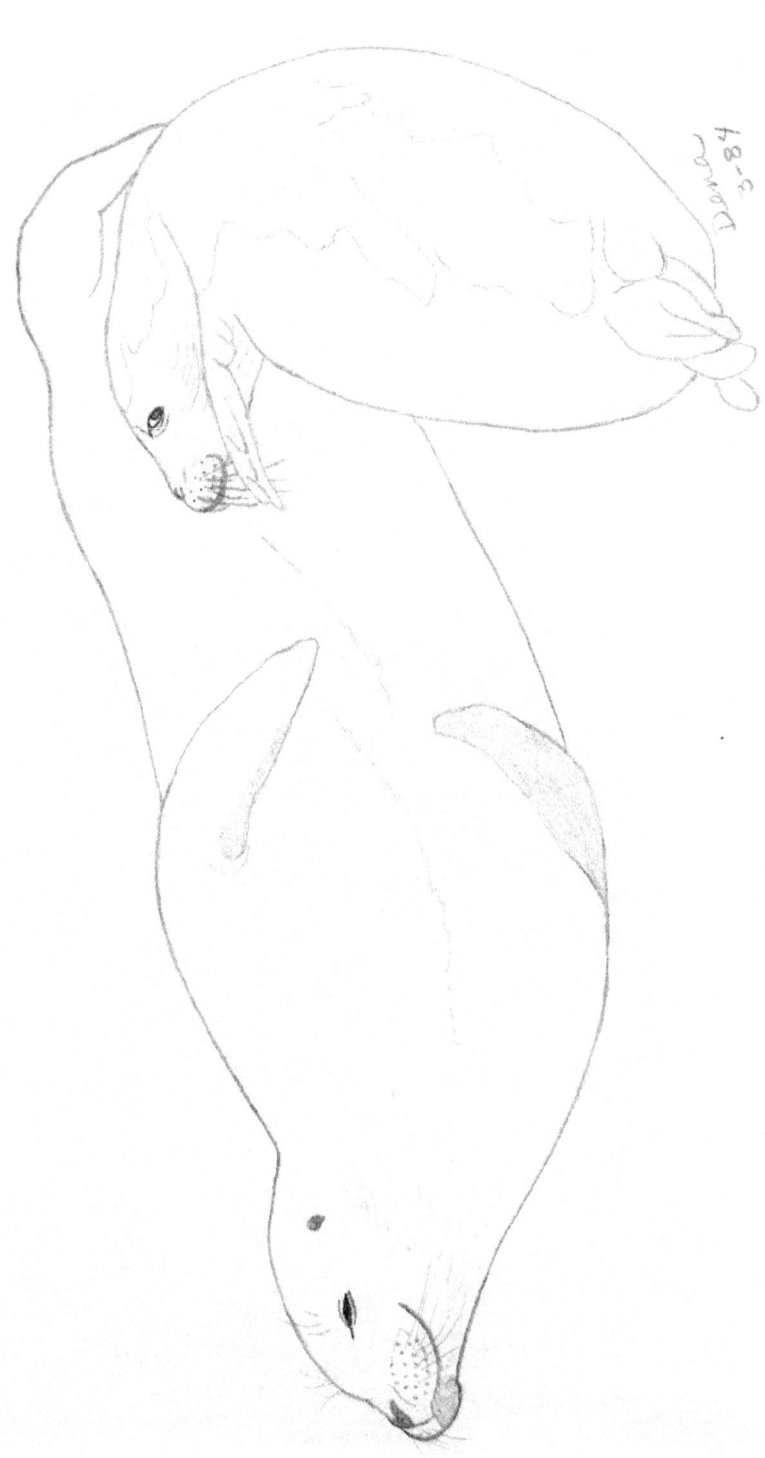

CHAPTER 7: Messages from New Zealand

From: Dena Matkin
Sent: November 11, 2001
To: Kirk Haskell
Subject: Funfunfun

If you are really traveling vicariously through us, you are having a great time! I was nervous enough to be very awake for my orca presentation at University of Auckland. Scott Baker said the students loved it, so I believed him.

Eve and I rented a car and headed to the north tip of the North Island last week. Cape Rienga was gorgeous. It is where the Pacific Ocean and the Tasman Sea come together, creating the biggest tide rip I've ever seen… miles long. We've been staying in little self-contained cabins for cheap, and taking short hikes whenever we feel like it. I think your friend Jim, on the sailboat *Response,* is no longer doing charters in the Bay of Islands, but we got on a neat 50-foot sailboat one day and sailed around with a Kiwi family that live on their boat and home-school their young son.

We are both ready to move to New Zealand. Scott and Anjanette have dual citizenship, as do their two kids, Kai and Neve. We are back at their place in Auckland now, reorganized (sending extra stuff home to lighten our load), and are heading out to the Coromandel Peninsula in our little car today. We hope to do an overnight horseback trip there, go to the Hot Water Beach, and stay in a hostel we heard was in a beautiful location. Then I think we're off to the South Island.

We constantly refer to the map you made of your past trip to New Zealand, which is great to have! I must admit when I hear old American music (they play it all the time here) I do get pangs of nostalgia. Maybe you could print out and send my e-mails to Mama so she can keep up with us and share with the rest of the family.

Willie arrives in Auckland November 20, and will probably meet us somewhere on the South Island. He and Eve and I will travel together for a week or two. He seems like a good guy, and easy to travel with.

Well, time to go get busy having more fun. We miss you and think about you every day. Your youthful spirit is still here in New Zealand and in our hearts.

Much love, Dena and Eve

From: Dena Matkin
Sent: November 18, 2001
To: Kirk Haskell
Subject: Morefunfun

Hi Kirk,

Good to hear from you, just letting you know you're still having fun. We're back in Auckland again, getting ready to fly south to Wellington and catch the ferry to the South Island. We're going to stay at a hostel called the Lazy Fish you can only get to by boat in Marlborough Sound. Hope to do some kayaking there, then on to Abel Tasman National Park. Most of the hostels we've stayed at have been really nice, in pretty locations, and clean, especially the one in Whitianga on the Coromandel Peninsula. So we have not set the tent up yet (except for the one time in your living room!).

We did a horse trek for a day on the Coromandel, great weather, then a little hiking and sunning on a white sandy beach the next day. We met a girl at the hostel who is from Fryslan in the Netherlands, where our Dutch ancestors lived. (You sort of pronounce it "Freezeland"). She showed us the patch on her backpack that is the symbol for that region, and I was so excited to see it.

I forgot to tell you that Eve saw her first penguin (the little blue) on our sailing trip in the Bay of Islands. I had never seen that particular one before, so I was thrilled. Needless to say, it doesn't take much to thrill me these days. We hope to see more penguins when we are in Dunedin, a good place to find them on a walk you can take. I'm going to rent a car to travel down the east coast, then up the west coast of the South Island. Hope to go out on a whale-watching trip off Kaikurra and/or Akaroa to look for sperm whales (a first for me and Eve if we find any), and possibly see Hector's dolphins (another first).

We've soaked in a few hot springs, and been on a few fast water slides, which is definitely wild and fun. Yesterday we hiked to a beautiful waterfall west of Auckland and had a picnic on the beach.

This trip will come to an end all too fast. Yes, time does fly when you're having fun! But it will be fun to ski with you if we can. I assume you picked up those pictures for me, hopefully they finally got it right.

We'll be in touch. Hope things are going well with your house-building plans.

Love, Dena and Eve

From: Kirk Haskell
Sent: November 19, 2001
To: Dena Matkin
Subject: Morefunfun

Hi,

I was hoping to hear from my Kiwi girls soon. Thanks for the great update on my vicarious vacation. It's good to know what I'm doing. I'm looking forward to a big picture show.

I finally picked up my plans from the architect last Friday. I will need about two weeks to do a final review and make corrections but I can start getting them out to subs to develop a realistic construction budget. Another step closer!

I picked up your pictures the day after I took you to the airport. I sent your previous e-mail to Mama and will send future ones also. She really likes getting them. Is Mount Cook on your itinerary? I thought it was beautiful there but the weather was rather gloomy.

Keep having fun. I'm looking forward to your return.

Much love,

Kirk

Postcard from Dena Matkin
To Doris Haskell
On December 2, 2001:

Dear Mama,

I hope you've been keeping track of us through Kirk. If you love sunsets, rainbows, sandy beaches and green rolling hills, plus extremely friendly people and a great money exchange rate, you would surely love New Zealand. I will be sending you some pictures after I get home. Today I sent you a little something for Christmas. What a treat to be spending this time with Eve as a friend. Today we took the ferry to the South Island, heading out by boat tomorrow to a hostel in Queen Charlotte Sound for some paddling. Eve's friend Willie is supposed to join us in about a week as we head down the east coast of the South Island, probably by car. I think about you all the time, especially when I see beautiful sunsets.

Love, Dena

From: Dena Matkin
Sent: December 4, 2001
To: Kirk Haskell
Subject: South Island

Dear Kirk,

Hope you haven't been worrying about us, but it's not always easy to find the time and place to send e-mails. Fortunately it is possible, though. I hope you are saving these messages, as they are sort of a journal of this trip, and I accidentally deleted my last one to you. I hope you got the postcard and small package I sent you. I just sent Mama another postcard she will get soon, as well as a Christmas card to Barb and her family. We still think about you all the time (Loved the iceberg picture!). Mama probably told you we called her from a phone booth at the end of a little pier out in Marlborough Sound where we were staying at the hostel you can only reach by boat. That night we went rowing out offshore there and saw some common dolphins leaping and playing in the distance.

After that we rented another little car in Picton and drove out to Golden Bay near Farewell Spit on the northern coast of the South Island. We stayed in a little cottage and did some day hikes on the beach. We found some New Zealand fur seals that were just hanging out on the beach. I photographed them as well as some cool fossils in the rocks. It's amazing the great pictures I'm getting with that little Olympus camera of Daddy's (I keep thinking, if only he knew what that little camera would ultimately see!). I don't think we'll make it to Mount Cook this time, but I'm planning on coming back.

We met up with Eve's friend Willie there in Collingwood, then did an overnight hike with him in Abel Tasman National Park (very rainy, but lush old growth forest beautiful), so we finally set up my new tent, and it works great. Actually, we've used it several times now, and are getting quite proficient at setting it up. We then drove on to Kaikura, where I wanted to go whale-watching. I met up with my naturalist friend Sean Neilson from Glacier Bay and he and I went out on a whale-watching day trip together… we saw both our first sperm whale and even saw a blue whale which is very rare. They hadn't seen a blue one for two months before our trip that morning, so we felt very lucky.

After that, Eve and I decided to keep traveling together until I have to leave in mid-December. She and I are very compatible traveling partners, and she and Willie will again travel together once I'm gone. Like Orion in the Southern Hemisphere, Willie has his feet planted firmly in the air. He is going to hitch-hike his way to Christchurch to visit old family friends. So, lo and behold, once again I am blessed to have my precious daughter all to myself, and we are having so much fun. We continued south down the east coast of the South Island, out on the Banks Peninsula, where we went out in this guy's little skiff and saw yellow-eyed penguins. Then some bow-riding Hector's dolphins came in really close.

We went through Christchurch one day, saw the city center statues, parks and street musicians, but being country girls we soon had to get out of that crowded city. In Oamaru, we saw more yellow-eyed penguins coming out of the surf to feed their chicks in the nests. We even got this old naturalist guy named Jim to take us right up to a nest containing a mom and two new baby chicks. Who should show up after that but Sean Neilson again, searching for his first penguin ever, and Eve and I were able to show him a yellow-eyed penguin striding out of the surf. Then a funny local guy showed us where we could watch a bunch of little blue penguins coming up another beach to their nests after dark. They are so adorable!

Then on through Dunedin (another too big, too busy city), to the Otago Peninsula where we saw the huge royal albatross. And we saw Sean once again, as he is on a similar mission to see wildlife unique to the Southern Hemisphere. Now Eve and I are at Lake Wanaka in the mountains where we may do some kayaking or more hiking. Eve would like to buy a used car before I leave her in about a week, so she can be more independent after I'm back in Alaska. I drop my rental car off in Picton before boarding the ferry for the North Island. Then I fly to Auckland, then as you know back to America the Beautiful and Eugene on December 14.

So this is turning into a novel. I'll have tons of pictures to show you when I get there, as I've been getting them developed along the way.

See you soon.
Love, Dena

The following is part of a longer e-mail Sean Neilson wrote from somewhere on the South Island, New Zealand to all his friends (including us) at the time he was traveling:

From: Sean Neilson
Sent: December, 2001
To: Dena and Eve Matkin
Subject: 10 pages from the South Island

...Eventually I pulled myself away and successfully made it out of town (Christchurch) and back to the highway south. The next destination would be Oamaru, in search of the penguins that I failed to see in Akaroa. Somehow, I managed to bump into Dena and her daughter Eve again, doing the same thing I was doing, searching for penguins. They had gotten there earlier than I did, but gave me the scoop on how to meet up with the Park Ranger (Jim) the next day. He was able to give them a close-up view of one of the most rare penguins, the yellow-eyed penguin.

At that point, there was still a little light left in the day, so they took me to a viewing area and with their help I was able to have a look at my first penguin. I know it sounds a bit weird, if you are not a bird-nerd like I am, but I was excited. Not like the Cleveland Indians winning-the-pennant-excited, but excited nevertheless. We ended up chatting with a local guy (Norman) who told us he would be happy to show us a place where another species of penguin, the little blue, could be spotted. Norman appeared to me to be a bit of a dodgy character at first, with cream-colored spiky hair and teeth that pointed every direction except for north and south. A wee bit skeptical, I followed him in our cars down to the water. He explained to Dena and I (the professional naturalists) all about global warming. It was good fun though, and he soon took off, leaving us to wait around for the penguins, which we did. Not long before dark, about a dozen or more little blues swam into shore, some of which appeared to get absolutely hammered against the rocks in the surf. However, much like when a young child appears to suffer a devastating fall, they just picked themselves up and scurried ashore to their nesting area, no worse for wear.

So, in the course of one hour, I was able to view TWO species of penguins. Great fun.

The fun continued early the next morning when the loud rapping of knuckles on my window woke me from a peaceful sleep. I assumed it was an angry farmer, making me move my wagon (I named her Charlotte by the way) off of his property. Well, if you've ever seen me right after I've woken up, you know I am not with it at all. Top it off with not having my glasses handy, made me all the more confused. After a minute or so of fumbling around, and noting that it was 5:17 in the morning it struck me that my unwanted alarm clock wasn't an angry farmer, but the indefatigable Norman! What was he up to? After a little more clarity reached my brain, I started guessing that Norman was trying for sympathy tips while guiding people to see penguins w/o a proper permit. He was trying to get me to go to the viewing area to see the penguins head out to sea. (While penguin pairs are nesting, one leaves in the morning to feed while the other tends to the nest. They come in during the evenings and then switch the next day, so the best viewing is really early in the morning, as Norman had told me the night before). Yet I digress.

I grabbed my camera and went down there. When I got down there and saw that Norman had rounded up four other unsuspecting penguin-seeking tourist, I was fairly certain what he was up to. No matter, I had no plans of giving him any money, and he was good entertainment.

About thirty minutes into our view, another man slinking around the bush at the edge of the beached, aimed a camera at our group and took a few photos. From Dena's description the day before, I recognized the man as Ranger Jim. I also recognized that he was there to document Norman schemes.

Ranger Jim and I had a good chat about Norman, but more about Alaska, birds and the rare yellow-eyed penguins he had been protecting for 22 years. Being a fellow ranger, he took to me straight away, and was kind enough to take me on a private penguin tour. He knows where the nesting sites are and showed me two of them. Surprisingly, the first nest was being tended to by both adults. They had two charcoal gray puffballs for chicks, which were at the feet of the female. The adults truly do have yellow eyes along with a yellow band that flows back horizontally towards the back of their head. They are amazingly tolerant of people, as I was only about three feet away. This will definitely be one of the things I'll always remember from this trip. As I was watching the two-week-old puffballs, one managed to take its first uncoordinated steps and nearly tumble out of the nest! It was a bit humorous and a real treat to have such an intimate window into penguin chickhood.

Ranger Jim apparently didn't have quite enough of Ranger Sean, so he invited me to his home for breakfast. I met his wife Dianna and enjoyed chatting over tea and toast. They even offered to let me spend the night, if not then, in the future perhaps.

Still traveling down the east coast, I left for the peninsula which juts out from Dunedin to view royal albatross. This is the only point in the world where they nest on the mainland. I wasn't able to see them in flight, but I did see them on a nest and I did get a look at their 10-foot wingspan as they stretched them out. I wasn't all that surprised when I came down from the viewing area to see, once again, Dena and Eve in the parking lot.

From: Eve Matkin
Sent: December 7, 2001
To: Dena Matkin
Subject: Safe and Sound

Dearest Mommy,

I am in Christchurch and checked into a BBH here. We got lucky hitching and got a ride all the way to Christchurch with a security guard. I have found lots of options here for buying a car and my friend Kyle is going to help me since he knows a bit about cars. We have been getting along great and having a ton of fun together. I am dead tired so I will write more soon. I miss you like crazy and love you more than anything in the whole universe. I will talk to you soon and hope everything is going well on your travels.

Love always and forever, Eve

From: Dena Matkin
Sent: December 12, 2001
To: Eve Matkin
Subject: Extremely relieved

Dear Eve,

I got your "safe and sound" message, but was a bit confused as it was dated December 7, the day I left you in Wanaka. (By the way, send me a copy of the *Backpacker News* if you are in it, OK?). Anyway, I know you were in Christchurch yesterday because I saw Hugh in Picton yesterday, and he said he'd just seen you about to buy a car there... great! You may have gotten my other "extremely relieved" message from Nelson Lakes if I pushed the "send" button in time.

I did a short hike up to the Franz Joseph Glacier after talking to you on the phone, and picked up a rock on the trail that had an "E" on it, so I saved it. During the previous night, while camping in my car, there was an earthquake for a few seconds, like at home.

I miss you every day, and hope things are continuing to go well. My drive along the Buller River (a neat river to raft, I think) to Nelson Lakes National Park was stunning. I stayed at the Yellow House Hostel there for two days so I could hike a bit. I climbed up Mt. Roberts above tree-line (really distant views and neat alpine vegetation) and got hailed on like crazy. It felt like Alaska for sure. (I was instantly homesick for Alaska the minute I left you).

On my drive there, I stopped and asked a farmer about the colors painted on the cow's backs. They are painted red if they are in heat, then blue if they get impregnated. Driving into Blenheim yesterday (nice place to shop), I saw the vineyard with the rose bushes planted in front of every row, and took the last picture on my last roll of film.

I stayed at the Picton YHA, which was a lot nicer and quieter than the BBH down the street. When I returned the rental car, they thought everything looked fine... whew! A lady in one of the shops in Picton told me there is a story about kingfishers... if you see one land, and make a wish before it takes off, your wish comes true!

Good news... I found a necklace at a jewelry store there that was almost exactly like the one you bought and gave away. I had the carver there change it so it looks exactly like the one you had! So it is now my Christmas present to you, the best friend I ever had. Do you want me to leave it with your stuff in Auckland, or do you want me to take it home and save it for you? And remember, really you are your own best friend!!!

I'm at the Wellington Worldwide Backpackers now, just got off the ferry, and going to the Natural History Museum tomorrow. I'll be in Auckland on December 13 for sure, so call me then so you can tell me what if anything to leave behind for you.

Till then, I love you always and forever, Mom

From: Eve Matkin
Sent: December 13, 2001
To: Dena Matkin
Subject: the best and loveliest mommy that ever lived

Dear mommy,

I am having a wonderful time with Kyle. I bought a car that I can sleep in the back of and runs great. It was $1,000 but well worth it. Kyle was so helpful and stuck by me through all my car ordeals. Well, I am in Westport on the South Island now and heading north towards Karamea which sound absolutely beautiful. Well, I will call you tonight and let you in on all the details.

That is so wonderful that you found a necklace for me. I have looked and can't find anything I have been happy with. It is even more special coming from you. You can't imagine how much I miss you, mom. Just reading your e-mail made me want to cry. You are the best friend I ever had and ever will have. I can't wait to talk to you.

Love always and forever, Eve

From: Dena Matkin
Sent: December 20, 2001
To: Eve Matkin
Subject: Hey Sweet!

Hey Angel Girl,

Got your message, and missed you more than ever. The evening I left New Zealand was so hard… the sunset was painfully breathtaking as I boarded the plane. It was all pastel of every color imaginable, and me with no film in my packed-away camera! But I will keep it in my mind and my heart forever. And I know you will take pictures of the most beautiful ones you see (I know you may miss a lot of those sun rises, though!). And, most importantly, I know I'll be back!

I left your necklace at the Bakers, along with the stove and my cooking pots (you may not want to use the "billy" that you bought because of the chipped enamel inside). For your info, the Bakers will be gone for sure the first week of January, so if you're passing through Auckland then you should let them know ahead of time, so they can leave a key out or whatever. They will be there for Christmas, though.

So tell me about Kyle… why does he have to leave so soon, where is he going, are you going to meet up again, where is he going to college, does he have a girlfriend, is he cute, etc, etc??? Wow, nosy Mom, huh? Oh, and Uncle Kirk wants to know what his future job prospects are! So did you find out more about school, honors program, etc? I wish I could help you from here. I'm in Eugene, going up skiing with Kirk tomorrow, then leaving Monday morning for home in Gustavus.

I hope your car is still going great, and I wish you could keep it there until I return. Sounds just like what I will want then. If you don't mind, could you tell me more details about it, just so I know what you are actually driving around in? What is the model, like does it have a name (no, I don't mean like "Charlotte"!). What color is it, what year is it, and what is the license number? One more thing, it would really be a smart idea to at least get liability insurance in case an accident was your fault. (OK, Mom, stop your damn worrying already!).

So, remember, I love you like crazy and think about you all the time, and hope most of all you are having funfunfun. I am now traveling vicariously through you, my precious Sweet.

Love forever, Mom

From: Eve Matkin
Sent: December 21, 2001
To: Dena Matkin
Subject: Hey…

Hey mommy girl,

I am glad you are safe back in the States and I am sorry you had to leave but I will take lots of pictures. Well, Kyle huh? He is very cute and has awesome curly hair. He is very into pottery and I have seen him do it at school in Homer. He is amazing. He has only been doing pottery for a couple years and it seems like he has done it his whole life. He is eventually going to college but going to travel a bit first because, like me, he doesn't know exactly what he wants to do with his life. He is also interested in marine biology and fish and game. He has to leave because he is going to Chile with some of his buds.

My car is a Toyota Corona station wagon. It is silver and I can't remember the license plate number but I will look at it later. It is running great, we had a slight problem with the radiator but got it to a mechanic who fixed her up for about $20. Oh, and she actually came with a name: "Good ol' Betty."

Well, Karamea was amazing and I got to do part of the Heaphy Track, which went to this beautiful sandy beach with a ravenous surf. Then we went and saw some rock arches that were so huge and some more exciting mysterious caves. There was also this lake called the Mirror Tarn which was like glass. Then we spent some time on the beach writing in our journals tanning. Well I am running out of time. I hope skiing was great. I wish I could have gone but I am definitely enjoying some more sun. Say hi to Kirk for me. I love you more than anything and am missin' you like crazy.

Love always and forever, Eve

After Eve flipped and totaled "Good ol' Betty," and Dena returned to New Zealand:

From: Eve Matkin
Sent: January 26, 2002
To: Dena Matkin
Subject: where oh where could my mommy be?

Hey Mom,

What have you been up to and where have you wandered off to? Willie and I are in Greymouth right now and are heading down the west coast of the South Island. We were thinking that a good place to meet up would be Wanaka on February 2 because we want to go to that Rippon Music Festival there. We might be able to meet before that but it depends on what you are doing. Let me know what your plans are and we can go from there.

I wrote Simone and let her know that you were coming and that you might give her a call when you get to Stewart Island. Also she works at the hotel restaurant so you could go and ask for her there and probably find her. Well I have to run but write soon so I know you are OK. Now I am being the Worry Wart. I miss you lots and can't wait to see you again.

Love Always, Eve

From: Eve Matkin
Sent: January 28, 2002
To: Dena Matkin
Subject: Write Me

Hey Mommy,

Just want to know where you are and when we are going to meet up. I hope everything is going good and that you are just having too much fun to write. I miss you lots and can't wait to travel with you again.

Love Always, Eve

From: Dena Matkin
Sent: February 3, 2002
To: Kirk Haskell
Subject: With Eve again

Dear Kirk,

Now, where was I? Oh yes, New Zealand! I hope you got my last message from Stewart Island just letting you know I'm fine, but since it was a bit short, I thought I'd fill in some of the spaces. At the moment I'm back in Wanaka, having met up with Eve and Willie here a couple days ago. (By the way, I loved the "winter postcard" photo of your land under snow!). It is very much summer here, feels a lot like August: HOT.

As I may have said before, Eve and Willie met me at my plane in Christchurch and we spent the afternoon at the incredible Botanical Gardens there. They took off and headed north the next day, and I spent an extra day in Christchurch so I could visit the Museum, which was really amazing with its bird and Antarctica section. I bought some of those multi-colored lupine seeds to try to start in my garden at home. That night I went to see the movie *Lord of the Rings*... did you know it was filmed here in New Zealand around Wanaka? You should see it, you really get a feel for what it's like here.

Next day I took a bus to Invercargill, then the ferry to Stewart Island the next morning. I did a hike from one side of Stewart Island to the other. You take a water taxi to the trail head, hike four hours, stay in a hut near the beach and look for kiwi birds late at night. It was on the full moon, very bright and lovely, and I found a kiwi that walked right up to my foot and sniffed my leg. (They have nostrils on the tip of their long beak). And in the sky just behind the kiwi, I could see the Southern Cross... wow, thrilled again! I stayed there two nights, hiked back over the Island, then from the water taxi back to the town, we saw bottlenose dolphins... another first for me.

I stayed at the same hostel that Eve had stayed in the town on Stewart Island. It was just part of this lady's house with a really pretty garden. Next day I headed back on the ferry to the South Island. Took a bus up to Te Anau, went past Lake Manapourri (really beautiful on a crystal clear day with the Kepler Mountains behind). I stayed at a backpackers hostel right on Lake Te Anau that night, then did a day hike up to Lake Marion off the road between Te Anau and Milford. It is a gorgeous little glacial lake up in an alpine bowl once carved out by a glacier with jagged peaks all around. You hike up beside a big rushing river through the rainforest to get there. I really did like Te Anau as a town more than Queenstown (which reminds me of a frantic anthill).

Since Eve wanted to meet me in Wanaka (there is a big music festival happening here), I headed up here, and was so glad to see her again. Still great sunny weather, we had a picnic by the lake and then Eve finally dragged me into the lake for a very refreshing swim. Yesterday I continued working on my tan, and we just had a nice do-nothing day. Today Eve and I are going back to Te Anau to do some more day hikes. You can get up to the Divide on the Routeburn Track if you hike about an hour uphill from the road to Milford Sound. You get some great views of the mountains and glacial valleys. Really nice to do without a heavy pack on.

Willie is going on his own to go cray-fishing with a commercial fisherman he met. Eve and I may head over to the west coast and hike up to Welcome Flats hot pools. There is a hut you can stay in next to the hot pools at the edge of the river. It is just south of Fox Glacier. Then back to Christchurch to get a rental car for our final two weeks here.

Eve may have told you she is going back to the U.S. as planned February 27, so she should see you in Eugene around then. We'll be in touch on that. She has decided to then go south to Mexico with her friend Eivin (from Homer) for the month of March. My flighty little precious girl.

So I'd better go for now. I'm using the New Zealand handbook you gave me all the time this trip… really coming in handy. Thinking about you all the time, I know you'll forward this to Mama and family. Thank you and love you all lots. It's so nice to have family somewhere when so far from home.

Love, Dena

From: Kirk Haskell
Sent: February 4, 2002
To: Dena Matkin
Subject: With Eve again

Dear Dena,

Good on ya! It's great to hear about places I've been. I can still picture many of them. I wish I was seeing the new places too. Can't say as I've ever had a kiwi sniff my leg. Glad to hear that you have temporary possession of Eve again.

It's really great to get your letters and I only wish I had more exciting news for you from this end. Keep it coming and have fun! (Stay left)

Much love,

Kirk

From: Eve Matkin
Sent: February 7, 2002
To: Kirk Haskell
Subject: Livin Life to the Fullest

Hi Kirk,

I am still having the time of my life in New Zealand and am soaking in the rays before I have to go home at the end of March. I have decided to go to Mexico for about three weeks with Eivin, Tocia and Holly which will be amazing because I miss all my friends so much. And it will be my first Third World experience.

I am in Wanaka right now which is a beautiful little town by a giant crystal lake with mountains all around. This is one of my favorite places in New Zealand. I swear it is paradise here. There are endless things to do, lots of sun, swimming and neat people to hang out with. It is going to be hard to leave NZ after all the wonderful days I have spent here.

Today I just did the most wild and crazy thing I have ever done in my life. I went skydiving. Yeah, I know you don't believe that timid Eve jumped out of a plane and plummeted to the ground from 9,000 feet in the air but I did. It just about made me piss my pants but as soon as I hit the ground I wanted to do it again. It is a feeling that I think everyone should experience once in their lives if they can.

Well I have to run but I just wanted to say hello and fill everyone in on my most recent adventure. Missin' ya all like crazy.

Lots of Love, Eve

From: Dena Matkin
Sent: February 8, 2002
To: Kirk Haskell
Subject: From the South Island

    Eve just sent you a message from Wanaka about her wild tandem skydiving adventure here yesterday, and I was right there on the ground to take pictures as they landed. Of course I was a nervous wreck, but we were both elated as she drifted down under the colorful canopy, laughing and calling "Hey, Mom!" all the way. I was finally able to show Eve the Southern Cross in the night sky, as the clear sunny weather has held for us. We've been able to swim in Lake Wanaka a lot, and we are both very tan. We did make it back to Te Anau last week, and did a wonderful tramp up to Key Summit on the Routeburn Track… jagged peaks in every direction, lakes (tarns), alpine plants and some lovely little mossy waterfalls on the way. I literally fell off the trail once looking at it all.

    Love you lots, Dena

From: Eve Matkin
Sent: February 28, 2002
To: Dena Matkin
Subject: Safe and sound in Eugene

    Hey Mommy,

    I made it safely to Eugene and I am very happy to be here. I didn't sleep for about 24 hours because I couldn't sleep on the plane, so it was a relief to fall into a nice cozy bed at Kirk's house. I am just unpacking and repacking at the moment, trying to figure out what to send home and what to bring to Mexico. I am so glad that I have a week to relax and get everything sorted out.
    So, how's everything going for you? Did you go to the caves? I'll forgive you if you didn't. I am so jealous that you are still in New Zealand and I'm not. I miss it so much already and I can't wait to get back. Well, I have to run. Kirk and I are going out to dinner tonight which should be nice. It has been a lot of fun telling him about the trip and comparing notes. I miss you like crazy mommy and think about you all the time.

    Hugs and kisses. XOXOXOX Lots of love, Eve

From: Dena Matkin
Sent: March 1, 2002
To: Kirk Haskell
Subject: Final NZ fun

Dear Kirk,

You have probably already heard some of the trip highlights in person from Eve, but I thought I'd send one more short journal before leaving this wonderful place. I will be home in Gustavus on March 5, so I'll likely call you soon after.

About two weeks before leaving New Zealand, Eve and I got the new (ha... more like rent-a-wreck!) rental car in Christchurch, and drove over Arthurs Pass since neither of us had been that way yet. We did a short hike up to some really tall waterfalls, then ended up in Hokitika on the west coast of the South Island that night. We stayed at a hostel that has two big bathtubs side by side in an outdoor enclosure where you can soak and look up at the stars at the same time.

Next day we went down the coast, and stayed near Fox Glacier that night at a Holiday Park that had "judderbars" (slow-down bumps in the road) at the entrance! Now suddenly judderbars are everywhere, thanks to you. Next day we did a six-hour trek up the Copland Track to Welcome Flats and hot pools. What a spot... up in a mountain range called the Sierra Range because they really do look like the jagged Minarets in the eastern Sierras of California. Gorgeous rainforest, lots of river crossings and suspension bridges.

Despite sore feet and backs (which did feel better after soaking in the naturally hot pools), we hiked back down the next morning, and drove on to Jackson Bay, south of Haast on the west coast. Right on the road near Jackson Bay we saw a Fiordland crested penguin just walking along, so of course we stopped and took pictures, which actually came out. I really didn't think we would get a chance to see this rare penguin, so we were excited, and hopefully didn't ruin its day too much.

We picked up Willie in Jackson Bay where he'd been commercial fishing with a cray fisherman, then we went on back to Wanaka. We always seem to end up here for the great weather, nice swimming and e-mailing you! We headed soon after to Christchurch and then traveled together for about a week. We went to an amazing local wine and food festival in Oamaru. Since it is on the east coast of the South Island, we were able to show Willie his first yellow-eyed penguins and first little blue penguins and his first view of the Southern Cross.

Then back to Wanaka, which is where Eve called Mama from a couple weeks ago. Mama couldn't believe she was actually talking to Eve... the last person she expected to hear from, so I was glad we called. Did you get a chance to hike up to the Rob Roy Glacier from the end of Lake Wanaka? We did part of the hike after camping at a really neat place by a river. You can jump into the freezing river from high up on a rock cliff, which we did again and again. Way fun, and we have pictures to prove our insanity.

We all drove back over to Jackson Bay, camped, then headed back up the west coast which remained under clear blue skies which is rare for that area as you know. Then back to Hokitika to experience the baths, and back to Arthurs Pass, where we camped in a spot so thick with sandflies they sounded like rain on the tent... terrifying! But it was a gorgeous glacial valley next to a wide beautiful river, nonetheless, that was enjoyable if you stayed out in a breeze strong enough to keep the bugs down.

We sent Willie on his way hitchhiking north to pick apples, and Eve and I went up to Mauria Hot Springs for more soaking. On the way, Eve took me to some caves she had found before that contained glowworms up on the dark ceiling. Next day we looked for and found a natural hot springs by a river, but didn't soak because the sandflies there were so thick I think they could have bled us dry in just a few minutes if we had removed any clothes.

Sadly, I had to say good-bye to Eve as she took a bus to start her journey back to America the Beautiful, and I headed north to Karamea on the west coast. What a place... I hiked the beginning of the Heaphy Track to the white sands of Scott's Beach. One very early morning I explored some huge limestone arches and dark caves as big as a house that had giant cave spiders (mating ones, no less!).

I continued back down the west coast so I could go back up the Copland Track to the Welcome Flats hot pools. Not quite as sunny as before. As a matter of fact, it rained so hard the rivers built up into raging torrents that were impassable. So people were stuck up at the Welcome Flats hut and pools for two nights until the rivers subsided enough to make crossings, and we were able to hike back down. Great Alaskan-type adventure!

So here I am in Wanaka again, touring and tasting at the local winery and beerworks. Tomorrow I hope to hike closer to the Rob Roy Glacier. Then it's back to Timaru, Christchurch, Auckland, LA, Seattle, Juneau, Gustavus, doggies and REALITY. The only way I can stand leaving is knowing I will return. You can't come back if you don't leave, they say.

Hopefully you will someday be here again. I've seen and done so much more here, but there is still even more yet to see and do. It never ends completely, just temporarily. I'll talk to you soon. Thanks for being there for Eve; she said it was so nice to be there with you.

Love you lots and lots, Dena

CHAPTER 8: Eve wisdom from Eugene, Oregon

College Essay By Eve Matkin (Age 20)

October, 2003
University of Oregon
Eugene, Oregon

In the center of the Alaskan wilderness, living the unique life that I have, has given me a perspective that has tinted my worldview, expanded me in ways that might never have been tapped into otherwise, and given me a deeper appreciation for all that life has to offer. Most importantly, these experiences have helped me to look beyond the material world that I believe drags people away from reality. Nature is an outlet for the imagination and a place where the mind is free from the grasps of society.

As a young girl, I grew up in a town of four to six hundred, the population fluctuating with the seasons. It was extremely isolated, and the only transport, in or out, was either on a four-seater bush plane or a small foot-passenger ferry that only ran during the summer. In the winter, it was sometimes impossible to leave. The town boasted one post office, store, gas station and school. I was immersed in an old-growth forest with wildlife literally on my front porch many days.

My mother and I lived alone, and I was always completely content with that. I never felt like anything was missing from my life except when I couldn't be with her. It seemed like my mother was always worrying about money, but I never remember lacking anything that I desired or was essential. Money was such an unreal idea to me because I never used it or had to deal with it. When I went to the store, I charged everything to our account so money hardly passed through my hands.

My mother is a naturalist and whale biologist, so she has instilled in me a passion for nature that will never diminish. I now see how at peace and euphoric it makes her to be drifting next to a pod of killer whales surrounded by glassy, calm water. The mountains protruding out with their razor sharp peaks that are capped with fresh snow, glistening in the brilliant sun. The smell of crisp ocean air intertwines with wafts of foul whale breath. All that can be heard is the sudden burst of life that arises from the ocean with their angular black dorsal fins quickly ducking below the silken water.

At one time in my life, I might have taken this kind of experience for granted, because this was the only life I had ever known. Whales were a part of the family and pristine beauty was my home. I was naïve to the idea that many people have barely seen the ocean, let alone a whale of any sort. Some people actually trap themselves in places where wilderness and natural splendor are almost impossible to find.

As I grew older and became more knowledgeable about the rest of the world, I realized that these experiences and places are finite. The natural world is being tainted rapidly and people are forgetting how to appreciate it. They are so distracted with the messages that society bombards us with, the greatest of which is consumerism to the highest degree. The message of the natural world cannot even get through the media's brain washing we absorb every day.

If there is no admiration for the environment, then there is no hesitation in its devastation. The earth no longer has the power to instill strong emotions in people because they are so detached from it. I have tried to absorb every light, texture, smell and sound of these unique experiences as if it could be the last. If we could all live every moment of our lives in this way, we would be an enlightened civilization. However, this may not be a realistic or practical way to contemplate these issues, but if people could, for a moment (with all of their being), I know they would be surprised by how it made them feel.

When I was sixteen, I went to live with my father in a larger town. I found that I could do things for myself and take responsibility for my actions. In my more complicated life, I learned to be more organized, focused and mature.

In leaving home, I had to learn to adapt to new situations and places. I went from being in a class of five students to a class of a hundred. There were more social groups and choices of friends who shared my values. I was overwhelmed by all of the people and social groups. I was very shy with everyone and very unsure of myself. However, the activities I pursued (choir, track and field, pottery and horseback riding) put me in the position to make friends.

Getting a summer job seemed exciting at first, and I jumped into it headlong. Soon I realized that working eight hours a day, five days a week, and bussing tables was not all fun and games. I quickly became swept up in the idea that I had to make money so that I could buy the material possessions my other friends had. Supposedly, I had been deprived of them. Consumerism had me wrapped around its little finger and I had so easily become blind to it. Eventually I began to feel discontented, like there was something missing from my everyday life. I began to consider what made me happy and I realized that I was only content when I escaped to a place that was void of all people. Surrounded by nature, I was at peace.

I began to go horseback riding every day so that I could pull myself away from the obligations of the life I had created. I would bring my sketch pad or journal and rip through the endless green fields below my house. I would just keep going until the land met the sea, and even then I would want to keep going across the bay that hugged the shores of my home, on through the endless reaches of untouched and unmutilated mountains.

My mind felt most free of all the constrictions of society in this place, and I could forget about the world spinning around me. This seemed like the only time that my imagination was clear enough to experience the crispness of every moment. I would bring the entirety of these thoughts home with me and it would allow me to interact with my family and society in a way that was healthy for my mind. I inter-mingled these two worlds to form a place that I could be content in.

Now I have been thrown into a situation that is dramatically different as compared to my upbringing. I live in the middle of a city that is beautiful but numbing. Although I quickly adapted to school life and the role of a "city girl," after a term I began to have a feeling of claustrophobia and a twinging need to leave. I slowly came to an understanding that I had to co-exist with society and to learn to see wonder and beauty in the urban world.

Money is a large factor in this society that can make things seem repulsive, but what is important is to come to an acceptance that there is so much to this world that is far beyond material possessions. We have to respond to and engage with the natural world as a solution to the excess of consumerism and to the preoccupation with money. With most decisions and actions, people should refer to the natural world because it is so heavily affected by humans and we by it. It can't be ignored for much longer. The world of humans and nature are entwined beyond separation.

Ignorance and alienation are preventing the recognition of this indestructible connection. If this detachment is pursued, then we will fail to see our responsibility for the natural environment. The earth's environment has the power to devastate humans and these illusions of money and consumerism that society has created will become completely irrelevant to the survival of the human race. There has to be ways found to more peacefully co-exist with the natural world.

Nature is a vital step in the reaching of human happiness and tranquility. There is a void that cannot be overcome by anything else but this beauty. Consumerism gives only a temporary feeling of happiness, but eventually leaves a person wanting more. It is an endless cycle that is only cause for more unrest because the true nature of this discontent cannot be found in the material world, but only in the natural environment.

A return to nature cannot always be done physically, but must be done imaginatively. People must learn to isolate themselves from society's environmentally unconstructive messages. This might be more difficult for some who have always been alien to the natural world and have not been privileged with a life as I have lived, close to nature. But I would hope that almost anyone can be reached by the awe-inspiring wonders the earth has brought forth.

CHAPTER 9: WHY ME?

In early 2003 I was diagnosed with Stage 1 breast cancer. I had gotten a routine mammogram, then traveled south to help my brother Kirk build his new house in the hilly outskirts of Eugene, Oregon. Being someone who rarely even caught a winter cold, who had birthed and successfully nursed a healthy daughter, who had moved to Alaska to live a more pure life, I decided that denial would be the best attitude to take.

I didn't want a lot of attention, any sympathy, healing-circle stuff, marches or pink flag waving. I wanted to get it taken care of and move on. Tight-lipped, level-headed, maniacally goal and detail oriented Kirk was the perfect companion. In between both of us continuing to work on his land and house, I went through doctor appointments, biopsies, procedures, tests and ultimately a double mastectomy. I decided on a breast reconstruction using the *latissimus dorsi* muscles brought forward from my back. They are the same muscles that help hold up a killer whale's dorsal fin, so I now affectionately refer to them as "my dorsals."

With my new mammaries, I could continue to study marine mammals just fine. I met a lot of very capable and kind health care workers and felt that I'd made new friends who were helping me get back home. At one point, my Iranian plastic surgeon took Kirk aside with the comment, "Your sister *really* wants to get back to Alaska!" Bright man. The intense longing to get back on my beloved *Kingfisher* and be with my astounding black and white friends again far outweighed the intensity of whatever pain and terror I was going through right then.

Kingfishers are small birds that have been thought to have spiritual qualities at least since ancient Greece. The species name for our belted kingfisher is *alcyon*: the god of calm water. All over the world, people have legends and admiration for these feisty and bejeweled little beings that symbolize peace, great love and dedication.

So with a heroic dedication, Kirk took care of me, we made great progress on his beautiful house and I was back in Glacier Bay by spring. My vanity was delighted that I didn't have to go through chemotherapy or radiation and risk losing my hair. I looked just the same and no one had a clue. Although Eve knew about it every step of the way, she decided on the denial route as well, and continued to get A's in all her college classes. She has always believed in my strength (even when I didn't) and that, combined with my mom's belief that I am a phoenix rising from the ashes, has always made me want to live up to their expectations.

It was also during this time that I finally took my mom's advice and began reading the books she had by and about the Dalai Lama. It didn't take long for me to come to the conclusion that he is the most enlightened being on the planet considering he is still tirelessly advocating forgiveness and peace after all he and his people have been through. I wanted to believe that if suffering was the path to spirituality, I should be well on my way. However, I knew in my heart it paled in comparison to that endured by the Tibetans and other oppressed people all over the world.

It was like a miracle in itself that I actually got to see the Dalai Lama a few years later. I couldn't believe we had both lived long enough to be in the same room together. My best friend Laurel had invited me there to Denver, Colorado, to be part of that group of thousands gathered to hear him speak his wisdom. The effect was so powerful that my soul felt cleansed by the tears that washed my face the entire time.

For a while, I basked in the illusion that a huge karmic debt of mine had been paid and that my life was spared from death by cancer for a reason. I did try to move forward in perpetual search for atonement for every stupid, fearful, selfish, wasteful, mean, angry, spectacular displays of poor judgment and words I had uttered in the past. I felt a new heightened urgency to give back to the world whatever knowledge and meaning I had gleaned from my brief existence. I further realized that the bars over the windows of my own prison were only over my eyes, and I ultimately made a long-overdue escape from a verbally and emotionally abusive relationship with the man I was dating at the time.

But why why why did this cancer happen to me? Are there even answers to this question? When were those evil seeds really planted in my body?

I grew up in a tiny desert town of about one thousand people on the eastern side of the Sierra Nevada Mountains, called Independence, California. At that time, the United States military was conducting tests over the border in Nevada in order to perfect the atomic bomb. Although they said that the wind blew all the fallout in an eastward direction (where breast cancer and miscarriage rates in some towns in Utah were truly in epidemic proportions), I am sure some of those radioactive poisons found their way that short distance west to me.

It was also during that time that mosquito eradication involved a truck going up and down the streets and alleys at night spraying DDT. It sounded like a huge monster with its deafening hiss as it passed our stone house and I remember how frightened I felt even though I knew what it was. I can also remember how much I loved the taste of dirt, never making the connection it was laced with a toxin so deadly it was eventually banned in this country. Later my family moved to the pesticide-saturated central valley of California, and even Alaska is not at all free from the toxic leavings of government and private projects.

The winter I took care of my mom in her home before we transitioned her into an assisted living facility, I learned a lot about the highs and lows of being a caregiver. The work itself was not all that hard… cooking, cleaning, getting her to appointments and to church. We sang in the choir together and I found books at the library we both enjoyed. The hardest part was maintaining my patience when her quirks drove me up the wall. Why? Because I saw myself in them! It is not always easy looking into a mirror.

On the flip side of that mirror, however, is a woman who deserves great respect for philosophies and convictions she held all her life. In finding an old college scrapbook of hers, I realized my mom was always deeply committed to the eternal concepts of non-violence, social justice and protection of our beautiful life-sustaining Earth. Her birthday is three days after Martin Luther King, Jr.'s (and eight years previous), and even before it became popular, she held dear all the cherished beliefs he lived and died for.

The real treasures lay in asking questions and learning more about my mom's parents and her childhood. Of all my ancestors, I think I identify the most with, and the tone of my life has paralleled, John and Grace de Wolf. John was the only grandparent I never met and so he became the most mysterious. He died of colon cancer in Michigan in 1952, three years after I was born. He was the original "Gypsy of the Family," having immigrated from northern Holland to Michigan when he was twenty-eight. Grace's grandparents met on the boat from Germany (there must have been a lot of hope on those ships!), and settled in Michigan.

John and Grace met at "some liberal meeting" in Detroit. After their marriage, they decided that they wanted to move to southern California and live on five acres of land. My mom calls them the original hippies. I can imagine their optimism as they headed west, baby Doris on the way. Grace became a first-grade teacher, but, out of economic necessity, John returned to Detroit to work as a machinist when my mom was only four. The marriage ended, but a small pile of letters John wrote at the time revealed a man in torment at being separated from his precious daughter.

As I read those letters late one night, John's spirit spoke eloquently to me a sad visceral message from across the years. For the first time, I really felt the sorrow Craig must have endured at being separated from Eve. Whatever grief storm I had going when I was left to raise a four month old baby alone in bush Alaska had clouded my vision of a man who had to live with a very hard decision.

One of John's letters was a page all in Dutch. In his careful long-hand, it has a title that says *Self Denial* and has six stanzas like a poem. It must have come from the depths of his soul to be written in the Fryslan dialect, his original language. Loosely translated, it is advice on the right way to live one's life. He wanted his baby daughter to become a good person and would have been thrilled to know she did. And now here I sit in "Freezeland, Alaska" attempting to impart the best of myself to grandchildren I may never meet. The first two stanzas sum up the gist of his translated original poem:

> *To deny oneself? Good.*
> *That is a noble goal.*
> *It is the ambition of a devout nature.*
> *For others hard to live with.*
>
> *But who wants to deny themselves,*
> *In words and in deeds,*
> *She will do it in good spirits, humble, quiet,*
> *And does not show her inside battle.*

Some of the things John had left behind, and mentioned in his letters, were oil paintings he had made. He was a very good artist, and wanted Doris to have them and remember him. My favorite had always been a small one of an old windmill next to a tiny stream in the flat Dutch countryside. In the foreground is an old wooden bridge and thatched hut; in the background, bright green grass and dark grey wind-streaked clouds. How deeply he must have missed that place at times, that place that had been his home. I wish I could tell him how much I love that painting, that it now lives in my house, and that his great granddaughter Eve now carries his artist gene.

When spring 2010 finally rolled around with pink and white blossoms raining down on the central valley, my mom was adjusting to her new life in assisted living. I had found her journal about her first trip to Alaska when she and my dad visited Craig and me in Homer in 1975. It was full of intricate details describing our cabin, the meals of Alaskan bounty we fixed for them, the berry picking, fishing and mushroom hunting, the chores of hauling water and hand-sawing firewood. *"Mama's Turnip Patch is a magnificent success! Wild berries of many kinds grow everywhere under foot... watermelon berry, nagoon, trailing raspberry."*

I sat alone in the California sunshine that drenched my mom's back yard, reading her nostalgic journal, listening to the sandhill cranes announcing they had had enough and were aching to return to their nesting grounds in Alaska. *Amen! Take me with you!* I spent a week in Homer with Eve and her partner Eivin on my way home to Gustavus. They have started a Community Supported Agriculture project there in Homer. It is a stunning extension of the hope and beauty that was her grandmother's original dream. In the rush of things, I had forgotten that I always compose a Valentine poem for Eve, so later I did:

> *Oh my goodness*
> *on Valentine's Day*
> *where was I?*
> *Being a poetic Mama*
> *with a tear of love*
> *in my eye?*
>
> *No, I was lost*
> *in the southland*
> *a land ruled by Mars*
> *too smoky and crowded*
> *to look up*
> *and see stars.*

*I was mothering
my mother
at times wondering why
so wrapped up in details
almost forgetting to notice
blossoms and blue sky.*

*Yearning for freedom
for a place that I love
wishing for playtime
with a daughter
who embodies
the spirit of a dove.*

*So here is
your Valentine
so heartfelt from me
thanks for the sledding
and wow
thanks for the ski.*

When Craig and I lived in Cordova, Alaska, I read *Where the Sea Breaks Its Back* by Corey Ford. It is the story of Georg Wilhelm Steller, the German naturalist who accompanied Vitus Bering on his fateful voyage from Russia to Alaska. Steller was the first European to discover and describe the plants, animals and indigenous people here. What he accomplished under unbelievably difficult circumstances in such a short amount of time has never been equaled in the field of natural science. Because of Steller, we now have a Steller's sea lion, jay, sea eagle, eider, albatross, greenling, invertebrates, plants.

He was thirty-three at the time, the same age I was when Eve was born. I decided that any child of mine would have Steller as a middle name, hence her name Eve Steller Matkin. Steller was brilliant, independent, spiritual, passionately curious, frugal and had a great respect for what we can learn from indigenous people. I also found I identified with some of his greatest character flaws: opinionated, tactless and unable to hold his sharp tongue. Fortunately, Eve is a little more positively evolved than I am in those traits.

My imperfections, pains and whines of "why me?" invariably begin to shrink in importance when I am confronted with the likes of the Dalai Lama, Martin Luther King, Georg Wilhelm Steller or John de Wolf. But it was a woman in the Seattle airport who brought inner toughness and struggle right into my face. As I waited in line for coffee, a small dark-haired shawl-covered woman appeared in front of me and asked if she could go ahead so she could get back to work.

She was sitting at a nearby table by the time I got my coffee, and she asked if I would like to sit with her. Through a rather thick accent, she told me that she was an Armenian refugee, now working pushing the people in wheelchairs around the airport. She, her mother and immediate family had first fled to Moscow, Russia. Eleven people had lived there in one room for four years.

As she related that fact, her eyes locked on mine, and as I looked into those dark pools of her memory, my own eyes instantly burned with tears. I was overcome by the knowledge of what she may have endured. I quietly sobbed and sipped coffee while she apologized and then related to me that her family now lives all together in Seattle, and that her other job is teaching piano. Which of course just made my tears cascade even faster. I thought about the musical talent she had brought with her to share in this new life in America. How many months or years might she have had to set it aside while she was just trying to survive?

I thought about the small oil painting I had carefully packed away in my daypack at that moment. The windmill, the green field, the bridge over the stream, signed J. de Wolf. I hugged my new Armenian friend as she left our table, she still apologizing for making me cry. It had become more of a smiling, laughing cry really.

Now whenever I find myself in the Seattle airport since that encounter, I search the faces of all the people pushing the wheelchairs of disabled travelers. I just have this crazy desire to know her name. I want to name a killer whale after her.

CHAPTER 10: Memoriam

April, 2006 / Gustavus, Alaska

    Last month my sister Barbara breathed her last breath and a look of peace and youthfulness finally settled on her face. Her life-long love and husband Bruce was by her side as my brother Lee sang her on her way. With part of my heart feeling forever broken, it was again time to fly south from Alaska to California to help our family celebrate Barb's 61-year life and memorialize her beautiful spirit.

    Flying south in the spring, against the flow of the birds migrating north, wing-beat by wing-beat, everything felt so odd. Against the slow motion rush of warmth and promise of new life another spring brings… no, nothing about going in that southerly direction felt natural or comfortable, exciting or joyful to this aging Alaskan.

    Well, good thing that natural feelings, comfort, spiritual excitement and joy come from unexpected places. Seeing my daughter Eve, who had driven from college in Oregon to central California for the occasion, connect with some of the offspring of other matrilines in our family tree… naturally, that was fun.

    The comfort and overwhelming pride that washed over me like waves as all the people who loved my sister in her daily life told me stories of how she had enhanced their lives… that was just plain amazing. The way her minister wove our family members' memories of Barb into a story of her life that made everyone laugh and cry, and by singing her favorite hymns… we all felt somehow uplifted.

    Getting to photograph my favorite aquatic animal (my mom Doris) diving, swimming and radiating good health during my visit… of course, brought relief and joy. Then, lo and behold, a little chance and a little planning conspired into another little road trip for Eve and me. We drove north through springtime coastal California and Oregon, with landscapes so reminiscent of New Zealand, "deconstructing" ourselves and laughing helplessly at humor only the two of us seem to fathom.

    The last time I talked to my sister Barb, it was actually she who made the effort, in her impaired condition, to pick up the phone and communicate with me. Maybe she knew it could be the last time we would be able to speak to each other. We both expressed how helpless we felt about her illness. I told her that she was the best sister that ever was, that she had made my life better in so many ways, and that I was going to dedicate my book to her.

During that last short phone call, Barb told me she remembered that she and I were best friends when we were growing up. She was my role model, I remembered. She remembered how hard it had been for both of us when she went off to college at University of California at Davis. Oh yes, I do remember that void inside me when she left, but I had forgotten what I did to fill that void. I wrote her letters, many many letters.

On his last visit home before the memorial, my brother Kirk had been rummaging through our mom's garage and finally opened a nondescript box he had been kicking around the garage floor since our dad's death eight years previous. And what was in that box? All those letters, many many letters that I wrote to Barb when I was still in high school and early college when I missed her more than my immature and insecure heart could stand. And more priceless treasures came out of that box when it was my turn to see it… fading black and white photographs taken when we were babies and children.

The most timeless letter that I found in that old box came out of a hot-pink (1960s-style bright colors inside) envelope with a letter I wrote to Barb after she had written that Bruce had to go to war in Vietnam. I was a sophomore at UC Santa Cruz and Barb was teaching Home Economics at Cal Poly in San Luis Obispo. February, 1969:

Dear Barb,

Gee… it sure was nice getting a letter from you. What a surprise!

I about cried when you said that about Bruce, though. Oh I do wish he didn't have to go, but who knows?… the war might even be over by then. Probably so. Things can easily change. I do hope so. But even if he does go, you have your diamond, and something fantastic to look forward to when he comes home. It really sounded cool when you said, "we'll be getting married…" like a beautiful dream come true!

So far as I know I'm still going to Hawaii this summer. Not positive about a job yet, but it'll work out, I'm sure.

I'm working now, as a matter of fact… wiping tables after dinner. (ugh!) Only $5.00 a week about, but it's money.

In case you haven't heard the good news... Butch knows where I am now. I don't know how, but he does. Oh, help! Help! Me Piglet! Piglet help!

Oh well, we'll just have to see what happens.

I'm liking classes pretty much this quarter, but sometimes I'm very confused about things. Not that I don't think it's normal... but I'm crazy!

Love, Dena

Yesterday the snow had finally melted off my garden here in Gustavus. I could hear the varied thrushes buzzing their calls like crazy and all the newly arriving warblers' songs filling in and advertising their cheerfully incessant need to make more life. When I woke up and looked outside this morning, it was snowing like crazy, covering everything and beginning to pile up on the spruce branches. It's supposed to snow for two days... the thrushes' calls sound a little less assertive. Well, at least I know I'm home... sure looks like home to me. Nothing like the promise of more cross-country skiing to cheer me up a bit.

Among their family vocal traditions, there are sounds that killer whales make sometimes that sound very much like high laughter "he, he." When I see a new wild killer whale calf with its yellow-orange eye patch, bouncing and rolling around its mom, nursing warm milk from her body in that ice-cold water, or doing headstands, it is easy for me to think that they could feel like laughing sometimes. I hope there are always things about wild killer whales that we fail to understand. I hope there are always clean wild oceans where they can retain their otherness, apart from the uncertain consequences of sharing this only earth with an even more dominant predator.

When we were older children, sister Barb first taught me how to play the ukulele and then the guitar. Our singing and playing together, besides long bicycle rides into the country, were what I missed the most when she went off to college. Maybe it's part of what she missed when I went off to pursue dreams in Alaska. Even now, playing the guitar, singing and maintaining our vocal traditions are the sounds that will always bind me to my family.

I took Barb out in my boat only once, but then she came to Gustavus only twice. We had a deep bond as children and with her being five years older than me, I had looked up to her for guidance.

She was an extraordinary teacher, cook, gardener, singer, guitar player and seamstress. She made her own very fancy wedding dress. She also made her matron-of-honor dress for my wedding. As adults we were as different as we could be, but that deep bond was always there, along with the music.

Traditional would sum Barb up in a single word, celebrating her wedding, loved ones' birthdays and Christian holidays in the most tastefully ornate and delicious ways possible. Miraculously enough, her beloved Bruce did return in one piece from the Vietnam War, they married and stayed married for 36 years, until her death. She never really understood my voracious love of traveling to new, beautiful and unique places in the world. And no matter how I tried to explain it to her, she especially didn't understand how I could leave my almost two-year-old daughter with my now ex-husband and go off for a month of learning and adventure in the Galapagos and Peru.

Non-traditional would be one all-encompassing way to describe me. After I had found and convinced the man/boy of my dreams to move to Alaska with me, I had to wait a year between my college graduation and his. While he finished a Biology degree at UC Santa Cruz, I impatiently waited, worked and skied in Yosemite. I had known since our first date skiing at Mammoth in the eastern Sierras, that I would marry Craig and have his baby or die trying. He and I left for Alaska together in June 1974 and although we returned briefly in 1976 for our outdoor wedding with college friends, there was never any doubt we belonged in Alaska. When our marriage ended and we began to reinvent our lives in late 1983, I was determined that my adventuring life was not over.

As I have patiently explained to my sister, mother or anyone else who might listen, I went to the Galapagos and Peru to continue fulfilling my dreams and expanding my exploring spirit. Feeling as if life was going backwards was not an option for me. I told them that the traveling actually made me a better parent in the long run. When I returned from my month-long adventures in South America in 1985, I felt enriched with experiences and treasures for *mi nina*, lucky to be alive and safe, and very very grateful to have a precious daughter to take care of and love.

Of course it had to be my fate to be detained and searched twice at the airport leaving Lima, Peru. The military had it surrounded with tanks and uniformed men with huge guns and machetes. I guess they decided I really was just a regular old hysterical mother who just needed to get back to her *nina* (I kept showing them her picture) in America. Promising myself never to return to anywhere south of Alaska, I finally ran across the tarmac, gasping for air to reach that last seat open on the plane to freedom. Back in California at my parents' house, Eve's initial blank stare soon turned into an effusive cascade of affection as we realized our good fortune at finding each other again.

Craig and I found our friendship again at the First Sitka Whalefest in 1997. Although we spoke about Eve and whales on the phone fairly frequently, we had not seen each other for about seven years. We were both in Sitka as speakers on our killer whale research, his in Prince William Sound and mine in Glacier Bay. Our deep common ties of past friendship, being co-authors of publications on killer whales and the presence of our then early-teenaged daughter made the redemption of forgiveness and renewed friendship seem as if it was the most natural thing in the world. Craig and I went back to our separate lives a lot more healed and whole.

The one and only time I took Barb out in my boat, she hadn't had much boating experience, and considering she was very timid about travel it was amazing she had made it all the way from her grape ranch in central California to the Bartlett Cove Dock in Glacier Bay. It was the day after her birthday in mid-July in the mid-1990's so I still had my first (19 foot) *Kingfisher,* an aluminum boat a lot more open and narrow than the second (20 foot) *Kingfisher* I now have.

Holding my hand, she crouched and carefully placed one foot then the other into the boat as if she expected it to tip right over. Still holding my hand, she groped her way to the seat next to mine and sat down. She held onto whatever was closest while I started, untied and moved the boat away from the dock and we headed out onto the calm mid-July morning water.

There were no killer whale sightings that day by us or called on the radio from anyone else. We motored slowly up to the Beardslee Entrance and turned off the outboard engine nearshore. It is a perfect spot to drift, eat lunch and watch for whales coming into or out of the Bay. Barb began to relax as we ate and looked out on the serene water surface with its stupendous island, mountain and glacier backdrop. We could hear humpback whales blowing all around the area, and I started noticing one of the humpback blows getting louder and saw one of them cruising our way close to the shoreline.

Barb stopped chewing her sandwich and gaped as the 40-ton adult humpback slowly surfaced nearby, exhaled loudly and continued on its way. We both sat in the boat in sheer delight of being in the calm presence of 40 feet of mammal. She really had nothing else in her life to compare it to, and I was thrilled to be able to give such a priceless gift to my monetarily-wealthy but wildlife-poor sister.

Later on, as we cruised back down to the Bartlett Cove Dock, Barb was completely relaxed, almost transformed. She sat in the front seat up in the bow, smiling as some of the afternoon chop came splashing over the bow, baptizing her with salty spray as we bumped along. Maybe she was connecting with memories of herself and husband Bruce when they used to go water-skiing with college friends. Maybe she was thinking farther back to when we lived in Independence, California, and she had a burro she named "Brighty" who gave fun and bumpy rides to us in the 4,000 foot high desert.

My memories of Barb as a child are elusive, but I think of her as being fairly comfortable around the water of streams, swimming holes in the desert, mountain lakes or at the beach. My earliest conscious memory is being with my family in a small rowboat on a huge lake in Idaho. The color and immensity of that much water was irresistibly enchanting to me, the three-year-old baby of the family at that time. Younger brother Kirk was yet to be born.

I remember leaning over and reaching my hands over the side of the boat, compelled to touch the soft cold velvet of the lake's surface. My older brother Lee nervously protested that I was going to tip us all into the water, and proceeded to spend his life as far away from boats and water, especially in its more frozen forms, as he could get. To his credit, he did pass a grueling Coast Guard basic training course. My basic attraction to the beauty of massive amounts of water, ice and snow continued unabated.

One of the reasons Eve loved Easter so much is because of Barb sending up treats and gifts from California for the Easter bunny to hide. Barb was our happy Easter fairy, and Eve and I developed our own family traditions and legends of Gustavus Easter times.

Easter by Eve Matkin (Age 12)

Easter is one of my favorite holidays because I love to find things, and I like chocolate and coloring eggs. Here is a short story that shows how my mom saved Easter. Well, me and my mom were sleeping. Then my mom woke up and looked out the window and she saw a raven. Then it flew up in the air and my mom saw a pink egg in its mouth. My mom went outside and tried to scare it away, and she did. Now my mom has to wake up really early and scare away the birds so they don't eat my eggs.

Then a few years later my mom found my same colored eggs under a log in the woods. I think the reason why the ravens got the eggs were because they were colorful and caught their eyes. I also think they didn't eat them because they were hard boiled and they didn't taste good to them.

Here are a couple of traditions at my house. First I wake up and I look for the eggs inside. Then when I get dressed I look for the eggs outside. When we come in we make bunny and Easter egg-shaped pancakes. When we finish eating we look at the things I got, and these are some of our traditions.

Easter is one of the best times of the year because it is when everything is just starting to grow and all the animals are just getting out of hibernating. I think lots of people would say they'd be glad that the snow would be gone, and I'm sure that lots of people would be glad to start working, too.

Well, that is what I love about Easter!!

CHAPTER 11: Dogs, bears and moose musings

May, 2007/ Gustavus, Alaska

About the time the dandelions and shooting stars are flooding the land and the pink and blue lupine are promising even more astounding color, the moose and bears appear with their fuzzy miniature offspring. Infinitely adorable young aside, moose and bear stories are not always love stories. In my world, though, everything relates somehow back to killer whales, and this is no exception. Both moose and bears species have had interactions with killer whales in the Glacier Bay / Icy Strait region. Most people in Gustavus probably have more moose than bear stories, in large part due to high moose numbers and the fact that moose are awake and present year-round.

It isn't insignificant that after 30-plus years of living in mainly black bear country in rural Alaska, I really have few bear stories. Trouble with bears usually starts with human mistakes. Or dogs. Your average bear just wants to mind its own business for the most part. But if you decide to put crab shells in the garbage in your shed, you may be surprised to hear the wooden slats of the shed wall being clawed and ripped off. Even then a sharp, "Hey, bear!!" usually sends them immediately on their way. And this human learned the valuable lesson early on of not leaving garbage of any kind within smelling distance of a bear.

When I worked for the Alaska Department of Fish and Game and then for the National Park Service counting salmon in streams, I found that bears well-fed on blueberries and salmon were rather content and harmless, just so you took care not to startle one close-up. My attitude became somewhat less blasé a few years ago, but it was because of that other animal element: my dogs. Historically there seems to be a deep and acrimonious relationship between dogs and bears. Just how acrimonious was brought abruptly to my attention as I rode my bicycle up the dirt driveway and into my front yard with black Labrador retriever Orca (male) and Remi (female) one fine sunny day.

I heard Remi explode into her deep ferocious bark before I even got there, then Orca joined in the fray, chasing and dancing back and forth with the extremely grumpy and scroungy-looking little black bear. Of course my job was to start screaming my head off at all of them. Oddly enough, no one was listening. At one point, the bear charged Remi, missed and planted its nose into the flimsy wire mesh of the garden fence. As if he wasn't mad enough before, now he was infuriated with this new pain.

The bright afternoon sun revealed brilliant red blood now coming out of his slightly torn nose. Somehow I got the dogs to come toward me and the woodshed. I bolted into the open woodshed, yelling and banging pieces of wood on the walls as the bear made a final charge toward us. Just a few feet away from the shed opening, the bear apparently decided it had had enough (I know I did), turned around and went to lie down under a nearby tree. It kept making growling and snapping noises and refused to leave, now completely unfazed by my growling and snapping noises.

One-by-one I had gotten the dogs into the adjacent tool shed with the door closed, then one-by-one ran with them over to the sturdy and high-fenced dog pen. The front door of the house was now closer, so again one-by-one I ran the dogs into the safety of the house. Sometime in the next few hours that poor little mangy bear left, but I didn't feel the same being outside for a long time. Later I heard the bear was shot while getting into someone's garbage. Some residents and visitors to Gustavus have still not learned the lesson that open garbage pits ultimately spell death for wild bears and more danger for people.

A few years later when I had become comfortable with bike-riding in the summer with the dogs again, I found myself in another precarious situation. It was an obviously bad combination of dogs, a delightful strawberry patch and a strawberry-loving mama bear. I had just stopped my bike and said to no one in particular, *Wow, look at all these beautiful berries!* When I heard the dogs barking agitatedly up ahead, I called them, then looked up to see Remi streaking toward me as fast as her long black legs would carry her. Close behind her a cinnamon-colored black bear was streaking along as fast as her stumpy cinnamon legs would carry her.

Continuing my obligatory screaming for the dogs to come and the bear to go, I jumped on my bike and pedaled as fast as my skinny white legs would pedal me ahead of the descending pack, Orca ultimately bringing up the rear. I saw later that this particular bear had a cub which is likely why she veered back into the nearby woods and I was able to pedal on home with my dogs and wait for my heart rate to slow down.

Because bears also swim, they occasionally come into contact with killer whales. The bear that interacted with killer whales was a large brown bear that was swimming across the entrance of Reid Inlet up the West Arm of Glacier Bay. Local resident Rusty Owen was in a kayak there that day in mid-June, 2002. As he watched, six killer whales, usually on the prowl for harbor seals at that time and place, approached and began milling around the brown bear. Sensing danger, the bear started foaming at the mouth as it continued its powerful swimming strokes toward the opposite shore. The whales got a good look, probably used their echolocation on the bear's huge bone structure as well as those sharp bear teeth and nails and moved on. The bear made it to shore unscathed.

Moose have an air of gangly silliness about them that can hide a real no-nonsense monster inside, at least as dangerous as a bear. The dogs seem to have respect for those long long legs equipped with hooves like sharp rocks. I am a bit wary as I cross-country ski. Sometimes moose choose to follow my ski trails, which help them get through the deep snow. Sometimes I see them standing out in the ditches, with just their wagging ears visible as they drink and feed in these sunken winter watering holes.

In the summer, moose are attracted into the yard by the fragrant magenta fireweed blossoms. From there they are attracted into the garden, which I now keep free of fireweed in hopes the moose won't step over the four-foot spindly wire fence to get to the rest of the garden goodies. One young male moose, having discovered this free bounty, decided he was going to spend the afternoon gorging on my greens. I strongly disagreed with him by telling him to leave, waving and banging a broom on things and making bluff charges from the protection of the dog pen.

The moose started to run away, then stopped and looked at me as if he had already in his vast experience gathered the impression that people were ineffective little creatures, all yelling and no follow-through. He approached the garden fence again. Finally in desperation I hopped onto the front porch and began my own stampede. I ran back and forth, yelling and stomping my feet hard and fast to sound like hot pursuit. I couldn't believe it, it worked! Ears flattened, hair up along his neck and back, head held high, the recalcitrant moose trotted off into the woods.

They do have their cute and curious moments, such as the time I looked out the front window to see one emerging from inside the dog pen. Fortunately the dogs were inside the house. I was able to take a picture before the more typical shyness of a wild animal urged it on its way.

Of course it would be a mama moose that would be the exception to any easy method for scaring moose out of the garden or anywhere else. In between two killer whale encounters on an early August day, I went home to put the remains of a freshly killed (by killer whales) harbor porpoise in the refrigerator to be dissected and examined later. I was extremely undelighted to find a large moose standing in the garden.

The four-foot long poles with small wire mesh in between is merely a suggestion to moose that they might not want to bother coming in. But no. The succulent pea plants, tops already chewed off by a previous visitor, were definitely worth the bother of stepping over the fence. Stepping back over the fence and out of the garden was not nearly so simple for this mama moose.

I grabbed my Coast Guard safety whistle and a few light sticks of wood. Blowing and throwing, I made bluff charges to drive her over the fence and away. She kept looking toward her young calf standing at a comfortable distance outside the fence. Junior looked back with an air of detached curiosity as if he just wanted mom to leave the lady and her precious garden so they could go off to the woods and have a nice nursing session together.

Unfortunately, his mom decided it was a much better idea to stand her ground in the garden. Moose in fight-or-flight mode have a maneuver where they turn to run away, then whirl around on their hind legs to face you, head down, ears back and a look of unbelievable malevolence in their eyes. By the time she was doing that dance, I was standing my ground on my three-foot high front porch which is just a few feet from the garden fence.

Mama moose came charging at me with her head near the ground and ears completely back, then stopped her half-ton bulk abruptly under the safety of the mountain ash tree, just spitting distance away. From the safety of my porch, I kept stomping, throwing sticks, whistle-blasting and glaring back at eye level with her. Maybe it was the distraction of her calf that kept her from leaping over the fence and sliding across the front porch and into my living room that morning. She finally jumped and turned away from the wood landing at her feet.

I was able to go open the garden gate for her to, hopefully, make a dignified exit, then, feeling anything but dignified, I went inside the house. When I came back out, she and her calf were gone along with every fireweed blossom that had beautifully and fragrantly lined my path. There was nothing for me to do but go back out on the water to track down the new killer whale sighting and be with marine animals much much higher on the fun and interesting scale.

Although swimming deer have made it onto the list of killer whale prey, it wasn't until June 13, 1992, in Icy Strait, that swimming moose made the prey species list. Many locals and visitors to this area have seen swimming moose. I have seen them in the middle of Sitakaday Narrows and other inlets inside Glacier Bay. Perhaps from being pursued by bears or wolves on the shore, they head into the icy waters for a new life on the other shore. They do have extremely thick skin and a thick mat of hair, but that cold water must sometimes take its toll on them.

Two locals, John Barry and Michael Opp, were in two separate skiffs, fishing near Pleasant Island Reef. The stories they related to me of the incident later were very similar: They both noticed two moose, the larger one in the lead, out in the middle of Icy Strait about a mile east of the Pleasant Island Reef Buoy. As they swam closer, it looked like a cow moose leading her calf by about ¼ mile. When she got to within about a mile of Pleasant Island, four killer whales approached her, splashing ensued, and she wasn't seen again. As soon as the splashing started, the calf moose turned back and swam toward a nearby kelp bed.

It arrived at the kelp bed just minutes before the four killer whales that were torpedoing toward it. As the struggling moose calf worked its way to the middle of the kelp bed, the adult male killer whale managed to work his way to within about ten yards of the moose before the whale leaped and shook himself free of the entangling kelp. The whale then swam around to the other side of the kelp bed, tried the same thing with the same results before jumping and shaking free.

Both times, the other three female and juvenile killer whales swam back and forth at the opposite edge of the kelp.

This coordinated effort had probably been successful in the past for them to drive harbor seals out of kelp beds. After about forty-five minutes of this, all four whales submerged at once, leaving the moose struggling and unable to free itself. Two days later, the carcass of a previous year's calf was found on Pleasant Island east of Long Beach.

There are times in life when one has to stop everything and think like another being or force of nature. Things whose habits and agendas become diametrically opposed to our own, consume one's entire sanity, outwit one at every turn: bears, moose, squirrels, bats, slugs, shrews, mosquitoes, porcupines, sickness, computers, rain, snow, tides, fire or human-induced melodrama, you name it.

But this is a book about love stories. Everyone has those THINGS in their lives, distracting us from our missions. Maybe those THINGS could be categorized as love stories because of the patience and perseverance they can foster in us. I have been lucky that my chosen mission to study the killer whales in my back yard always gave me the inspiration to endure the distractions and stay on my path.

A killer whale is the best friend one could ever want: loving the freedom of the wild seas, full of surprises and fresh ideas, a good communicator, devoted to family, likes to share, is funny, and each has that eternally forgiving smile. Anyway, it is a lot more fun to talk and write about killer whales. Having given me so much from all the accumulated brief glimpses I have had into their lives, I want to share the essence of those experiences.

CHAPTER 12: Killer whale love stories

Offshores

The first and only time I was with offshore killer whales was September 8, 1989. About thirty whales were spread out between Homeshore and Hoonah, traveling east in Icy Strait, divided into eight sub-groups. I estimated eight adult males total, and ten juveniles or calves, the rest females or immature males.

It was the most rag-tag bunch of whales I have ever seen. They had many large nicks along the trailing edge of their dorsal fins as if they did battle with sharks in order to obtain a meal. I thought about when Craig and I commercial gillnetted for salmon in Prince William Sound and once caught a six-foot salmon shark. We had to bring it on board the boat to disentangle it from the nylon mesh of the gillnet. Its skin was like the roughest sandpaper you could imagine, its mouth full of large sharp teeth. The offshores' teeth become ground down to the gum-line from eating so many rough-skinned sharks.

The other things I noticed most about the offshore killer whales were the rounded tips and slight bends in the ragged dorsals and the many scratches in the grey saddle patch just below each dorsal. One adult male kept doing something I still don't understand: at every surfacing, he would lean way over to the right, surrounded very closely by females and young. Injured? Playing? What?

Two same-sized immatures had very falcate (curved like a hook) dorsal fins, similar to the resident ecotype of killer whale who also eat fish. Residents and offshores are closer genetically to each other than they are to the transients, the ecotype that preys on marine mammals. We have begun to refer to these three ecotypes as distinct "cultures" as their food habits are passed down from one generation to the next.

The offshores are the rarest killer whales seen in the inside waters of southeastern Alaska because they are usually found farther offshore in the open Pacific and Gulf of Alaska. They are sometimes seen in groups several times the size of what I saw. It shouldn't have been such a huge surprise when, five years later (from August to October, 1994), one of the individuals I photo-identified in Icy Strait became trapped with eight other offshores in Barnes Lake on Prince of Wales Island near Ketchikan, Alaska. They may have been chasing salmon in with the flooding tide, but lacking experience in the tides of the area, didn't leave when the unusually high tide went out. One adult female and one sub-adult male died in the brackish freshwater lake during their seven week ordeal.

Eventually, the remaining offshores were driven out of Barnes Lake by rescuers in small boats herding the whales by making underwater noises to the lake exit during a very high tide. As I watched the rescue on local TV, I could see the whales group up as they made it out the narrow exit. The relief, joy and gratitude of all involved spread to me watching at home in Gustavus. Then, as if to accentuate the moment, I gasped at the TV in disbelief as I saw a rainbow appearing over the whales swimming toward the open sea and freedom.

My one and only encounter with offshores in 1989, however, left me feeling quite differently. The thirty-plus whales were spread out over the width of eastern Icy Strait, all heading toward Chatham Strait, away from Glacier Bay and home. East of the Sisters, with a dwindling gas supply, I left having approached maybe half the animals, not knowing at the time that this odd-looking, odd-behaving group was a new type of killer whale entirely. These feelings of confusion and ineptitude often followed me home in the years on the water. Not fully realizing that when all the pieces were put together with the other researchers, our insight would follow.

Residents

Mercifully, there were encounters with resident and transient killer whales when my eyes and my mind stayed open, the fuel and food lasted, the camera shutter clicked at all the right focused moments and I immediately knew what I was observing. And, mercifully, there were encounters that caused me to laugh all the way back to Bartlett Cove, safe inside the entrance to Glacier Bay.

Residents and transients are called sympatric ecotypes, meaning they live in over-lapping habitat along the North Pacific coast, but do not interbreed and do not eat the same food resources.

Many people are confused about the terms resident and transient killer whales, especially here in the Glacier Bay region of southeastern Alaska where small transient groups are the most commonly seen ecotype (genetically distinct form).

The concept of at least two separate killer whale types was grandfathered in British Columbia by the late Michael Bigg in the 1970s. Concurrently, Ken Balcomb was working down the Pacific Coast in the Puget Sound region. It was astounding how much the residents resided in patterns predicted by summer salmon movements, and the less predictable transients really did just transit through, often in winter months, and ate marine mammals.

Farther north, here in southeastern Alaska, the resident AF and AG pods are catalogued in *Killer Whales of Southern Alaska* by Craig Matkin, Graeme Ellis, Eva Saulitis, Lance Barrett-Lennard and Dena Matkin. In the spring, the residents follow king salmon traveling along shorelines from the outer coast of the Gulf of Alaska to the spawning streams of the inside passages. Late summer to fall can be a good time to see the residents following silver salmon through Icy Strait and all the way up to the glaciers of Glacier Bay. The residents are here looking for fish in the winter as well. There are white king salmon that stay in the Icy Strait area during winter months that the residents may have known about before people did. Residents often forage in smaller sub-pods of ten to twenty animals. They travel together in close family groups called matrilines, consisting of grandmothers and mothers with their sons and daughters.

Residents and transients generally stay separate, and only twice in twenty years I have observed transient killer whales following a group of resident AF whales. Why and how often this happens is still a mystery. The first time I saw it occurred in Icy Strait on August 19, 1992. A sub-pod of fourteen AF whales was traveling rapidly southeast in line-abreast formation, all side-by-side in a line. At Point Adolphus they all turned northeast, and crossed the width of Icy Strait to the south shore of Pleasant Island. Some of the calves were lobtailing by hitting the surface hard with tail flukes, and spyhopping by sticking their heads out of the water to look around. As they traveled, milled and rested before moving toward the salmon jumping around Pleasant Island Reef, I noticed two transients, one adult male and one younger male, following the same course as the residents. The two transient males always stayed a distance of at least a quarter mile for about three hours.

Ten years later, on July 8, 2002 eleven members of AF pod, including calves, were traveling south very slowly line-abreast in Glacier Bay. When I put the hydrophone in the water to listen, there was no vocalizing from the whales. Two hours into the encounter with the residents, a group of seven transient females and young began following about 100 yards behind the AF group. Less than an hour later, the transients hurried by, passing the residents and heading away to forage closer to shorelines. The residents continued their southerly course, more tightly grouped than before.

One of the most intriguing questions we'll likely never fully answer is how aware are wild killer whales of their power to delight and surprise us? Or make us laugh out of control? The sight of the two-foot long pink penis of a displaying adult male killer whale can most definitely evoke all that and more. Awe to the point of completely missing the camera shot most times.

Late in the day on August 24, 1992 was classic early-fall weather with wind-driven rain and one- to three-foot sea swells. A sub-group of AF pod was behaving too erratically for my getting decent left-side photo-identification. At first, the twelve whales were all together heading south toward Point Gustavus, out of Glacier Bay and into Icy Strait, where the white-capping seas promised only more challenges. Ignoring the salmon that jumped in the water ahead of us, the AFs all swam over and surrounded me. Bow, stern, both sides, the twelve whales were within a foot or two of touching the nineteen-foot aluminum boat.

I immediately took the outboard engine out of gear to stop the spinning propeller, and we all momentarily drifted along together. Instead of feeling intimidated, I felt hugged, briefly accepted into the splashing chaos of their freedom. The group became a large flower, a semi-solid mass of gentle breaths with my boat and me at the center of these breathing petals of blubber. When the whales started to disperse, I put the engine in gear again. Again the pod returned and closely surrounded me with spyhops and lobtails. One juvenile surfaced alongside belly-up displaying an erection, then quickly rolled over and dove as I burst out laughing.

As we traveled nearshore, the juvenile males lagged behind the main group. I could see them rolling over and over, foot-long pink penises flashing above the waves. Their upside-down lobtails were sometimes in perfect synchrony. Finally the adult male broke free from his female companions in the lead, came back and joined the frolicking juveniles. Then as if he had the last word on size, his considerably larger erection rose above the breaking waves. This definitive display over, he then rejoined his mom and the other southbound females leading the group out of the Bay. I laughed and hooted all the way back to Bartlett Cove. No amount of rain, poor photos and gathering darkness could quell the lingering warmth of that pod-hug or the humor of the male contest.

AG pod is the other commonly seen resident pod in the Glacier Bay area. Having seen one surface next to me with a halibut hanging out of its mouth in 1992, I dubbed them The Halibut Eaters from the beginning. In 2004, a few AG pod females and young were photo-documented attempting to take a halibut from a sport-fishing line in Icy Strait, only letting go of their half-eaten fish prize when it was reeled to within a whale's length of the boat. Present in southeastern Alaska every month of the year, AG pod occasionally travels north across the Gulf of Alaska as far as Kachemak Bay, another halibut hotspot at the west end of the Kenai Peninsula.

Both AF and AG pods travel from the Glacier Bay region to the Prince William Sound region and back on a fairly regular basis. They are capable of making the trip in a matter of just a few days, demonstrating an ability to travel more than 100 miles in a day.

In three separate cases, twice in May and once in October, I observed AG pod members milling and porpoising with small groups of Dall's porpoise for up to half an hour. The killer whales never attacked the little black and while porpoise, and both species appeared more interested in pursuing the small (about 3-inch) schooling fish that erupted periodically at the surface.

Pursuit, aggressive play and kills of harbor and Dall's porpoise are not typical resident behaviors. That is normally in the realm of transients. Very rarely, residents cross that invisible line. On July 19, 2002 one of the adult males in AG pod had control of a harbor porpoise as he lagged behind the main pod leaving Glacier Bay. The tide was ebbing against a building westerly wind which caused one foot swells to quickly become three to four foot breaking waves. For twenty minutes I managed to maneuver the boat, photograph and peer through binoculars at the unfolding scene.

I could see the resident male chasing, turning, rolling and shaking at the surface. He carried the little gray porpoise in his mouth, released it then chased it again. I thought I heard high-pitched squeals when the porpoise was mid-air. I had seen transients give similar treatment to harbor porpoise literally for hours, and I knew it could continue indefinitely. Rough seas prevented me from seeing the culmination of that one-sided game. I don't know how much more he prolonged it, or whether or not he finally made a meal of the terrified, possibly injured porpoise.

Another case of AG residents behaving like transients involved a common loon, which is a beautifully patterned black-and-white heavy-bodied bird. At the height of the flooding tide on October 2, 1992 I found a sub-group of seven AG females and young milling at the mouth of Glacier Bay's Bartlett River. This is a good time and place to find silver salmon schooling to head up the river to spawn and die.

The killer whale group soon headed south toward the entrance of the Bay. Close to the shoreline off Halibut Point, they scared up a pair of common loons, which flew about 50 yards then landed again on the water just outside the near-shore kelp beds. Some of the whales followed and began closely milling around one of the birds. It flapped and splashed at the surface when the whales dove underneath it. Within minutes, all the AG females, juveniles and calves were continuing south, leaving the calling loon for me to approach and assess. It tried to fly away, but only managed to flap and run along the sea surface to escape, possibly injured from a little rough play.

The whales continued on in major play mode: trailing kelp off their dorsal fins and tail flukes, slapping their dorsals and flukes on the surface, spyhopping, some juveniles and calves breaching clear of the water and splashing loudly back down. One juvenile with a very hooked dorsal fin approached the boat three times vocalizing so loudly I could hear it without a hydrophone. What wisdom was he/she expressing, I wondered? One cow/calf pair swam in unison on their sides a few feet underwater right next to the boat. I reached out my hand to them, tried to make eye contact and smiled.

R pod is a northern resident pod commonly from British Columbia. All or parts of R pod may sometimes be found in Frederick Sound, Chatham Strait or Icy Strait in southeastern Alaska. I was with R pod only once; they were in Frederick Sound and AF pod was swimming nearby. The most distinctive thing about R pod is that one of the adult males has a dorsal fin curved like a banana, looking like it was put on backwards. The tip of his dorsal fin curves toward his head.

Transients

Transient killer whales have been further divided into four separate populations: West Coast (Bigg's) transients whose highest numbers are found in British Columbia and southeastern Alaska, Gulf of Alaska transients who are found along the outer coast and northwestern Gulf of Alaska, the AT 1 (Chugach) subpopulation in Prince William Sound and Kenai Fjords, and the Western transients that hunt Aleutian waters. They are currently thought to be genetically distinct populations, but the scope of their inter-relationships is still being defined.

The first Gulf of Alaska transients I documented in Glacier Bay were two adult males AT 30 and AT 32 on July 19, 1998. They were traveling steadily south together along the western shoreline of Sitakaday Narrows, the almost two-mile-wide opening through which all boats and large marine mammals must pass to enter or exit Glacier Bay National Park and Preserve. Nothing in their path caused the two males to pause or investigate. They passed by single, seemingly vulnerable, sea otters floating within their grasp. They passed by mom and pup sea otters and groups of over 50 sea otters as if they weren't even there. They passed by humpback whales within a quarter-mile with no visible interactions. At Point Carolus they left the Bay, heading west toward the Gulf of Alaska.

The next time I saw AT 30 and AT 32 coming into Glacier Bay was June 5, 2001 in the company of another two Gulf of Alaska transients AT 74 and AT 74A and ten West Coast transients. Thereby those four AT whales may ultimately enter into the West Coast transient community by virtue of association. This further blurred the line between the two populations, and illuminated the need for continuing research.

That auspicious encounter in June of 2001 was made even more interesting by the presence of my female black Labrador retriever Remi. Vigorous and excitable are two of Remi's most noticeable traits. After two of the killer whales lunged toward a fleeing Steller sea lion, we stopped to see if it was still OK. Yes, it was just fine and the large adult sea lion then decided to check us out by circling, rolling and surfacing next to the boat. Its huge bulging eyes took in Remi with her front paws up on the back of the boat as if it was time to go for a swim.

I decided to pull my dog back from sure doom and continue to do my job of trying to photo-identify the transients and figure out what they were interested in eating. The transients, too, seemed to take a keen interest in my high-strung dog and me. No matter how I maneuvered *Kingfisher* to be on their left sides for proper catalog photographs, the whales kept approaching us head-on and line-abreast. Finally I gave up and let them maneuver and do whatever it was they were trying to do with us.

The tightly grouped transients proceeded to make a very close circle once around the boat, all surfacing in unison. By this time Remi had become completely unglued and it took all my strength to hold her back and keep her from leaping into the group of oogling whales. Having gotten an eye-full, and probably an ear-full as well, the transients went into resting behavior. They moved away and grouped tightly line-abreast facing a strong ebbing current. They made five minute submersions so slowly they drifted backwards together. It was a long time before I invited Remi to accompany me in the boat again. The years have mellowed her only a little, but the comfort of dog warmth becomes a precious thing in a cold open boat.

West Coast transients are the groups of killer whales I encounter most frequently here in northern southeastern Alaska. They generally forage in small assemblages of a half a dozen individuals, groups often consisting of several matrilines. Adult male transients sometimes choose to hunt alone or in vocal proximity to females and young. In late June/early July each year I have come to expect to see a transient super-pod of a minimum of 20 animals coming into Glacier Bay. This is a bit of a contradiction in terms because we usually refer to residents as being in pods and transients being in groups whose associations are more fluid and varied.

These large transient aggregations provide opportunities for social bonding and possible mating among matrilines. It is never exactly the same transient individuals, but I always recognize some of the distinctive adult males. After entering Glacier Bay, they spend the following days divided into smaller groups that hunt all the way to the glaciers of the East and West Arms where newly weaned harbor seals are starting to disperse.

The largest group of transients in Glacier Bay was a group of 35-plus mixed individuals on July 13, 2003. My mom and I escorted them from south of the Marble Islands, north to Tlingit Point, halfway to the glaciers. It was one of those deceptively calm and sunny days when one is far enough up in the Bay to be protected from the afternoon southwesterly winds. It is easy to forget about the full moon pulling at a huge ebbing tide and that this is the recipe for white-knuckled adventure on the way home.

The whales were traveling north in loosely-formed sub-groups. I recognized some of them as my regular transients, individuals I look for at this time year after year. T 85 was there with her two offspring, born three years apart. The distinctive low notch on her dorsal fin was the first thing I noticed about her when I first met her in 1988. She is the only killer whale to be photo-identified in Glacier Bay every year since. Being the first known female, she naturally became the Eve of my study.

Adult male T 87 and female T 88 were there as well, the long rectangular notch near the top of his dorsal easily seen at a distance. Although their exact genetic relationship is unknown, they have always been seen traveling together throughout their more than 20 year history in Icy Strait and Glacier Bay.

As the group of 35 transients swept past the Steller sea lion haulout at South Marble Island, about 30 sea lions that were in the water at the base of the haulout arched their necks toward the passing killer whales. About 50 more growling and agitated sea lions started jumping into the water from the safety of the high smooth rocks, and began porpoising rapidly toward the retreating whales as if it was a fine afternoon for an interspecies rumble. There are no sea lion pups at South Marble, just large adults with teeth, nails and a feisty attitude.

North of the Marble Islands the transient sub-groups began joining into a larger group, the juveniles actively playing and noisily slapping their tails on the water. Good thing I had already photographed T 87 and T 88, as they had already slipped away, possibly continuing north into the peaceful calm of the East Arm where plentiful harbor seals and harbor porpoise hold the promise of many fine leisurely meals.

The rest of my afternoon, however, proved to be anything but peaceful. Checking the tide book I saw that it was mid-ebb, meaning that all the water that had been pushing us north up the Bay now was pouring south out of the Bay through the constricted Sitakaday Narrows. When relatively shallow seas are coming from one direction and hard afternoon winds are coming from the opposite direction, tide rips and large breaking waves result.

As we headed south down the Bay, I could see the whitecaps building into a big washing machine effect up ahead. Strong piece of advice: make every effort to not run over even the smallest piece of kelp with an outboard engine. When I heard the overheat alarm go off, I knew I had to stop the boat, back up to expel any kelp from the water intake, then turn off the engine to cool it down and stop the alarm. During the few seconds this took to be accomplished, the *Kingfisher* was pulled rapidly south by the tidal river. After turning the engine back on, it was cooled enough so the alarm stayed off and I looked up to see two giant smooth swells taller than the boat. We went over the first swell, disappeared into the trough between them, then up over the second one.

Telling my 80-something-year-old mom to hang on tight (no need to tell her that, standing there beside me with her hands wrapped around the railing, her knuckles already white), I pushed the throttle down and we angled across now-breaking six-foot waves along Young and Lester Islands toward Bartlett Cove. Thankful that this new *Kingfisher* has a cuddy (partial) cabin, we didn't get wet by any of the water breaking over our heads.

Keeping a death grip on the steering wheel, I thought about how this wasn't even the worst I'd seen. I'd been in this exact spot many years before in a small open skiff with even bigger waves when I was coming back from a bird survey. As always, not making it home was not an option, and as my stable *Kingfisher* surfed into Bartlett Cove, I turned to my wide-eyed mother and remarked what a fine boat we had to bring us and the priceless data back home. She spoke of little else but those crashing waves for a very long time to anyone who would listen, and tried to make me promise never to be out in such conditions ever again. When it came time for another whale survey a day or so later, without hesitation she climbed back into the boat and off we went.

There is another large distinctive dorsal fin I search for in those transient aggregations each year. T 2 is an adult male I first saw in 1986 in Icy Strait, and I have now known him for twenty-seven years. The tip of his dorsal curves down tightly to the left, looking like an upside-down umbrella handle. Seen from the right side, the top looks chopped off. When the British Columbia researchers first photo-identified him off Canada ten years previous, his dorsal was all upright. Fortunately, his saddle patch had long scratches across it, so a match was made.

Since they hadn't seen him for so long, he was thought to have possibly died, but he became one of Glacier Bay's regular visitors. Graeme Ellis eventually reorganized the transient designations, and T 2 became T 40 in John Ford and Graeme Ellis's catalog *Transients: Mammal-Hunting Killer Whales*. However, the name T 2 stuck as one of those Glacier Bay legends. By then he had terminated so many harbor seals and been recognized in the area by so many people that his motto had truly become, *I'll be back!*

I have seen T 2 with many of the transient females and young, and associations between the transient adult males and maternal sub-groups can change literally from one day to the next. I usually see T 2 in the company of T 85 and her offspring several times between spring and late fall. Again, we do not know their exact genetic relationship, but they, too, have been consistent hunting partners over time. T 2 is one of the adult males who occasionally prefers to hunt alone. He disappears for hours into Wilderness Waters I cannot follow him into with an engine. Fascinating and fun as it would be to join him, I find myself rejoicing at the fact that there are places in Glacier Bay where a transient can forage in utter peace and quiet, free from even the prying eyes of science.

Unfortunately for transient killer whales, eating marine mammals isn't always a matter for rejoicing. Being at the top of the food chain makes transients more vulnerable to the effects of pollutants. Toxins from the ocean environment accumulate in the fat tissues of seals, porpoises and sea lions when they eat their fish diet. These toxins then become even more highly concentrated in the blubber of the whales that eat these other marine mammals. Creating protected habitat is a great start, but protecting a seemingly invincible whale such as T 2 becomes part of a global challenge to clean up our oceans.

Harbor seal predation

One of T 2's hunting techniques, besides being alone and silent, is to take his time debilitating a seal by repeated smacks from his tail flukes. Hunting partners take turns lobtailing on seals or quickly sliding past them to feel the prey's texture on their sensitive skin.

Sometimes they peel the skin from their prey and trade-off carrying the bloody remains in their mouths or tear it apart to share.

Seals react to such terror in various ways. They can hide deep in the thick kelp beds to escape visual and acoustic detection as the transients forage as close as physically possible to shallow shorelines. Some seals, and sea lions as well, attempt to climb into boats or onto swim steps of boats to escape. Welcoming a marine mammal into one's boat is to be avoided. They look adorable to us, but they are wild and all are equipped to be fierce and dangerous if confined.

In an encounter with T 2, the target seal came near my drifting boat with its huge eyes looking at me as if human companionship would be the preferred option. In an instant T 2 came by and whisked the seal away under water, never to be seen again. In another encounter, a seal actually opened its mouth and snapped at one of the attacking whales, still scrappy even though it was trapped in a hopeless situation.

During a harbor seal kill on July 18, 2005 by cow T 99 and her two-year-old juvenile T 99A, the small seal appeared paralyzed, floating at the surface and just looking at the slowly milling whales. When a kill is in progress, my usual strategy is to stop the boat, turn off the engine and put the hydrophone in the water to listen and record any sounds. I keep cameras and dip-net ready to collect photos and any prey remains.

This was one of those encounters when people are likely to think, "Gee, why do transients have to be so mean?" The best answer to that might be: to pass hunting techniques from one generation to the next through repetitive play and practice. I think of transient behavior as being prolonged enthusiasm with survival benefits. After about ten minutes of pursuit, T 99 and T 99A began taking turns surfacing slowly with the seal in their mouths.

The whales lobtailed, rolled and lunged at the surface whereupon the cow T 137 and her juvenile T 137A joined the first pair. Over the hydrophone, the whales began making sounds like clapping, loud whining calls, low growls, then one of the transients made a piercing up-sliding scream. That last loud call seemed to announce the kill, as the seal was permanently gone from the surface after that. All four whales immediately continued north on their way together up into Glacier Bay.

Dall's and harbor porpoise predation

Porpoise can stimulate even more of that prolonged enthusiasm in transients. They are fast, agile and more capable of escape than seals, so porpoise present a bigger challenge for a killer whale to eventually subdue. I see more harbor than Dall's porpoise kills because I work most often inside Glacier Bay. The farther into Icy Strait I venture, the more Dall's porpoise I encounter, and therefore, increased kills of Dall's by transients.

One of the most remarkable harbor porpoise events did happen far outside Glacier Bay, west toward the Gulf of Alaska just outside Dundas Bay. I was still just getting to know the male T 87 on July 7, 1994. After that day, it seemed appropriate to name him Harbeson after an independent old-timer who had lived off the land in a cabin inside Dundas Bay long ago. T 87 was the only adult male with ten other West Coast transients: besides T 88, who has never had a calf with her, all females with their young. When I arrived on the calm sunny scene, they were in three separate groups.

In hindsight, they may have already killed and eaten a mother harbor porpoise, and they appeared to be in resting mode. The T 124 group was all oriented in the same direction, heads at the surface, blowholes closed and quite oblivious to my presence. In later years I named T 124 Myrtle as in Fertile Myrtle because she has produced five healthy calves, all born between three and six years apart. Her daughter T 124A has subsequently given birth to T 124A1, T 124A2, T 124A3 and T 124A4, so forming another separate hunting group.

T 85 and T 86 were also present with their first-born juveniles at the 1994 Dundas Bay encounter. They were a little more active than the resting group about one-quarter mile away. They milled about together, but completely ignored a lone sea otter drifting in a nearby tide rip. T 87 and T 88 were together about one-quarter mile to the west of the others.

Within thirty minutes, the three sub-groups were joining and heading first southwest then turning around to head northeast. It was then that I noticed there was a focal point to the group: T 87 had a still-living baby harbor porpoise swimming next to him. It was little more than a foot long with a white belly and lightly mottled gray back.

For the next three hours T 87 played gently with the baby porpoise as he swam slowly in a large clockwise circle with the remainder of the transients behind or beside him. None of the other whales ever handled the porpoise. As far as I could see, it was his toy to roll around with for the afternoon. Sometimes its little tail would be splashing out the side of his mouth as they submerged together. As he surfaced T 87 would scoop his tail under him, as if helping to bring the porpoise to the surface again.

Sometimes it was swimming ahead of him, and once it rolled over his back the way killer whale calves play with their mothers. At one point the tiny porpoise was high and dry, riding on top of T 87's huge head. Through the hydrophone I could hear loud echolocation clicks and calls rising to a higher pitch. At the end of three hours, the game still seemed in full swing, but there was no doubt in my mind how it would end. With the day ending, the wind rising and far from home, I left the baby porpoise alive but probably not so well.

Like seal prey, porpoise can also get passed around among group members. In another debilitating move, transients send porpoise flying through the air with a whack of their tail flukes. Instead of eating porpoise in one easy gulp, transients eat the skin and nibble on the inch-thick blubber layer that lies just between skin and muscle. Juveniles then can take their time eating more or just practice handling the remains.

They occasionally leave behind the floating porpoise lungs, and after examining that slimy spongy lung tissue, I tend to agree with the transients that this may not be the tastiest tidbit. I am particularly delighted when I arrive at a kill to find a whole skinned porpoise skeleton, face intact, with just the tail, blubber and meat nibbled off, insides falling out. To be honest, I've never really relished the blood and guts aspect of biology, but I can't help but admire these multi-ton whales' delicately perfected techniques.

Steller sea lion predation

The primary impetus behind increased killer whale funding in 2001 was the building awareness of the Endangered Steller sea lion in western Alaska where population numbers were crashing. Here in southeastern Alaska, Steller sea lion numbers are stable or increasing, so they are listed as only Threatened, meaning they are in less imminent danger of becoming extinct. Although there are rare cross-overs, the eastern and western Steller sea lion populations are considered separate, so they can be scientifically compared.

It is truly amazing how quickly such a complex problem as the decline of a marine species can be blamed on killer whales. Many species of fish, birds and marine mammals, including killer whales, may never fully recover from the incalculable decimation from the oil spilled in Prince William Sound in 1989 that spread its toxic death west toward the Aleutians. Other factors, such as climate, sea changes and commercial fisheries had added to the complexity of the western Alaska ecosystem long before the 1989 oil spill played its part. The only good news about the oil spill is that it never came southeast to contaminate the relatively pristine waters of Glacier Bay National Park and Preserve. After 1989, for me Glacier Bay and the rest of southeastern Alaska became an even more priceless and irreplaceable treasure to protect and study.

When you think of a healthy Steller sea lion, imagine a huge, tough, rowdy, social, curious, sleek bear (teeth, claws and all) cruising gracefully through the ocean. In groups, sea lions exude fearlessness. In a small boat or kayak, I would much rather be surrounded by transient killer whales than a group of adult male sea lions. During an encounter with residents in Icy Strait, I noticed a stray group of resident juveniles rushing over to rejoin the main pod. A little way behind them, a small gang of sea lions were craning their necks toward the fleeing whales. I wondered how the sea lions seemed so confident they weren't going to be attacked by the fish-eating whales.

Seeing even the mammal-eating transients mount an attack on an adult sea lion has proven to be a rare event in my experience. There is always much easier prey to be had in Glacier Bay and Icy Strait. It is quite a challenge to subdue a sea lion fighting for its life, but Charlie Chin was a transient male equal to the challenge.

I first met him in 1989, and the unique shape of his broad-based dorsal fin left quite a lasting impression. The trailing edge near the top of his dorsal looked like it had a bite out of it, so that the very tip was like a finger sticking out. He became T 1 when the Transient Catalog came out. The British Columbia researchers named him Charlie Chin because his lower jaw protruded in its own uniquely abnormal way. He may have died by now as he hasn't been sighted since the mid-1990s.

He was very much alive on June 29, 1990, milling with two females and a calf in the tide rips off the Beardslee Entrance inside Glacier Bay. One of the first things I noticed was splashes from the whales breaching on a young sea lion that was thrashing at the surface. One of the transients then took it down long enough to either drown or bite it to death because soon it floated quite still at the surface. Now safe for the calf to play with and eat, the cow and calf took the dead sea lion under for the last time. Charlie Chin proceeded to lobtail, breach and roll around with an erection between the kill site and me in the boat. All of them began spyhopping to get a better look at me, and one female lunged and breached in such a way that the majority of waves and spray came toward the boat. I took that to be an emphatic *Back off our kill!* as sputtery vocalizations came spewing out of her blowhole when she surfaced nearby.

No problem; there is no real doubt in my mind as to who is in charge in these situations, and it is never me. For the next hour or so until I left, I kept a respectful distance so I could observe transient behavior without influencing it. The calf remained excited, rapidly porpoising at the surface and breaching while the cow spyhopped to monitor their surroundings above the surface. Eventually the four joined up again and headed into the Beardslee Entrance together. Content with my new photos, thrills and insight, I was more than happy to leave them in peace.

More typically, transients ignore or just harass sea lions. The adult male T 72 exhibited similar behavior a few years later by breaching at me while the females and young in the group were milling around a sea lion close to shore. I noticed fresh cuts and scratches on T 72 that made me think he had just had his fill of battling something. Again, I took the breaching as a territorial warning, and I waited as patiently as I could until the group went on, leaving the sea lion alive and apparently unhurt. When I approached to check on its condition, it looked at me wild-eyed from the safety of a near-shore kelp bed.

The Steller sea lions one sees in Glacier Bay tend to be full-grown adults that are here to safely rest and feed. I was a bit surprised to see the T 68 group, seven in all, harassing a half-grown sea lion on July 21, 2004. As I headed north from Flapjack Island toward South Marble Island, I saw a lot of surface activity which often signifies an attack is in progress. The transients were taking turns quickly swimming past and also leaping clear over the frantic sea lion.

I stopped the boat, turned off the engine and put the hydrophone into the water, anticipating a lot of vocalizing since they already had their prey and there was no more need for stealth and silence. I wasn't disappointed. My boat had just become the closest island, and the sea lion swam over and looked up at me as if I was its new best friend. At that moment, one of the whales emitted a whine that sounded just like, *Aw, shucks!* As they repeatedly circled the boat looking at their prey hiding underneath, the transients continued to vocalize with high whistles, echolocation clicks and calls that are similar to the sound of a rooster crowing.

Unlike my experience with transient male T 2 taking a harbor seal hovering near the boat, the T 68 transient group stayed about a whales' length away from the boat. They never attempted to snatch the sea lion out from under the bow of the boat. Their attention span for this game was less than an hour and they eventually disappeared into Wilderness Waters to practice their skills.

Seabird predation

Like transient attacks on sea lions, attacks on seabirds don't always conclude with a meal. Seabirds such as mergansers and scoters molt some of their feathers and become temporarily flightless mid to late summer. Predation rates on seabirds in Glacier Bay may be higher than in other areas due to the fact that there are many calm bays and inlets where the birds can gather and feed, protected by regulations that ban boats with engines at biologically sensitive times. Female transients and young use the opportunity for target practice. I have yet to see a wild adult male killer whale play with or eat a bird.

Flightless or injured seabirds provide the perfect opportunity for young whales to practice chasing, hitting into the air, lobtailing or breaching on birds, and playing catch and release. Murrelets and murres are birds that spend a lot of time just floating on the surface, making dives to catch small schooling fish. Once caught by a transient cow, the injured bird can then be repeatedly brought back for her calf to hone new predatory maneuvers as the prey runs and flaps across the surface or dives to escape.

I responded to a sighting of a group of seven transients (T 2 / T 40 included) on July 11, 2003. They were spread out as they slowly traveled south over the reefs between Boulder and Strawberry Islands, down Strawberry Passage toward the inside of Beardslee Entrance. The many humpback whales in the vicinity wheezed loud drawn-out exhales, began lightly slapping their tail flukes or headed in the opposite direction when the killer whales passed too close. A gang of five sea lions and a single sea otter porpoised rapidly toward the safety of the kelp beds along the eastern shore of Strawberry Island. The two youngest juvenile transients were charged with energy and as they began milling among some nearby mergansers, I stopped and put the hydrophone in the water.

It often seems that there is more vocalizing in killer whale groups that contain young whales, and this was one of those times. They began chasing the flightless mergansers back and forth, around in circles and into the rocky shallows of Strawberry Island. One merganser disappeared into a huge toothy mouth as I recorded the whales' loud high whistles, up-sliding calls, buzzes and popping sounds. The low-pitched grumbling sounds most likely came from the nearby humpback whales. Another merganser was caught, released, then left behind, wounded and dying beside the boat. I barely had time to feel a little sick at its suffering before the bird put its head underwater and exhaled a few final bubbles.

By then, the whales had charged off and the females and young surrounded a humpback cow and calf who thrashed their tail flukes side-to-side and headed closer to shore. T 2 patrolled back and forth on the outside edge of the action. Soon the transients all joined into a tight group, line-abreast and made their way slowly southeast into Icy Strait, surfacing in unison with regular five minute dives.

Minke whale predation

As captain Andy Spear began a day of whale-watching in Icy Strait on July 27, 1996, he had no idea that before the day was over he would be witnessing one of the most rare predation events to be seen in this part of the killer whale world. In his own words from the log of his sailboat *Adventuress*:

A pod of killer whales attack a minke whale. We were heading into

Glacier Bay when the whole group of them came charging right at us. What we thought was an orca in the lead turned out to be a minke whale. Just as they got to the boat the lead male orca hit the minke and there was a great deal of thrashing and blood in the water. Then the big killer dove with the minke and resurfaced lifting the minke. The lead orca had two distinct notches in his dorsal fin and it was in an "S" shape.

This went on for nearly two hours as two young males leaped about, they accompanied the male leader in the foray. Meanwhile just outside all this was another large male moving very slowly around the action, but never participating. There was one group that looked like five females that stuck together and moved in and out of the action. Much later, another large male appeared. While all of this was going on, a humpback (a big one) moved into the area and the lead orca charged and rammed it. The humpback turned over and there was thrashing about, but no blood. This was repeated three times and the orcas left the humpback alone. The humpback did not leave the area but continued to surface, maybe feeding. Finally the whole group seemed to dive and we didn't see the minke again. It appeared to us that this was a sort of a training session for the young males. All pretty intense and surrounding the boat. We didn't even have to move to see it all. I called the Park Service to inform Dena Matkin about all of this and she came out to photograph them.

When I finally arrived on the scene, the minke had sunk just south of Point Gustavus in 120 feet of water. I photo-identified thirteen transients as they dove and milled in the huge whale-oil slick and the chunks of white whale blubber floating around. T 63 was the dynamic adult male leader of the attack. With those two distinct notches near the top of the trailing edge of his dorsal and his wild determined behavior, he became known as Zorro after that day. T 87 Harbeson was another one of the five adult males. The youngest I identified was three year old T 65B Chunk, there with its mother T 65 Whidbey II.

Humpback whales

The phenomenon of humpbacks approaching to observe transients killing other species has been reported to me from several sources. The most fascinating video I ever received was from visitor Craig Kellogg, a passenger on board a small tour-boat drifting west of Point Adolphus in Icy Strait. It started as an attack by six transients lobtailing repeatedly on an adult Steller sea lion.

About fifteen minutes into the attack, four adult humpback whales not only approached but began to participate. They took many turns swimming closely past and it appeared that they were slowly lobtailing on the floating sea lion. One of the humpbacks actually reached out with one of its six-foot long pectoral fins (like our arms) and touched the dying sea lion.

The killer whales would allow the humpbacks' approach temporarily, then would rush in to give the sea lion renewed and harder tail slaps. At these times I could tell that the humpback and killer whales were passing within a whales' length of each other under water. The humpbacks' exhalations would become loud and drawn-out wheeze-blows and their tail flukes slashed rapidly from side-to-side. The transients never seemed to attack the humpbacks, instead focusing on killing the sea lion. After about fifty minutes of these interactions the three humpbacks left the scene together.

I can understand the humpbacks' curiosity about transient predatory behavior, getting to know the enemy is important, but this was even more intriguing. It made me think about all the times I'd seen sea lions harassing and nipping at humpbacks. Could this be a display of humpback aggression toward the sea lion; the not so gentle giants just taking advantage of a rare opportunity? About a decade later I observed a pair of humpbacks swim rapidly up to a floating pile of sea lion intestines that a group of transient killer whales had left behind from their kill. Much to my astonishment, the humpbacks began lobtailing on the floating sea lion remains! Part of the beauty of this work is the mystery of it all, and the fact that we will never know what goes on in their minds.

Sea otter predation

Transient killer whales have frequently been blamed for the demise of sea otter populations. My observations for almost twenty years have led me to believe it is most common in Icy Strait and Glacier Bay for the two species to ignore one another even when in close proximity. Sea otters are the largest members of the weasel family, have almost no body fat, so have to groom to keep an insulating layer of air trapped in their thick fur. Not an ideal item for the killer whale menu.

When my friend Ingrid Visser, the New Zealand Orca Lady, was visiting Alaska in 2003, she and I saw a transient killer whale knock a sea otter aside with the side of its head and swim on. The otter, stunned at first, quickly recovered, dove and went on its lucky way. The incident seemed to characterize the typical transient attitude, *Get out of my way, you stinking sea weasel!*

The next year on July 10, 2004 I finally saw four juvenile transients, aged three to eleven years, harassing a sea otter. Similar to their attacks on seabirds, I believe this event had more to do with target practice than obtaining nutritious food. I photo-identified a total of 28 transients that day between Strawberry and Boulder Islands, but only those four juveniles participated in the sea otter attack.

They took turns leaping over, rubbing their flanks past the otter that was lying on its back, paws together as if in prayer, or taking it under only to have it reappear at the surface, vigorously shaking its head. It seemed as though the juveniles were trying to hit the otter with the side edge of their tail flukes, more difficult but potentially more destructive. I don't think they ever really connected with it, but it was making crying sounds and trying to groom. Through the hydrophone the transients were making up-sliding calls, high whistles and chirping sounds.

I started feeling a little sick as it became increasingly difficult to watch. I've always had a soft spot in my heart for those adorable otter faces. The adult male T 63 Zorro stayed nearby, swimming back and forth, observing, maybe making sure I was behaving myself. Trying to be the good impartial scientist, I didn't interfere in any way.

Finally the whole group left the area, the juveniles abandoned the otter and I went over to check on it. By then it acted as if it just wanted to sleep floating on its back. It woke up long enough to look up at me, dive and swim through a kelp bed and go back to sleep close to the north shore of Strawberry Island. Since it hadn't been able to groom and insulate itself from the cold water for over an hour, it may have ultimately died of hypothermia.

During the summer of 2006 I found three dead sea otters, none of which had died from killer whale predation. On August 11, 2006 my black Labrador retriever Remi sniffed out a dead sea otter on the Gustavus beach. It became the first case of valvular endocarditis (later identified by U.S. Fish and Wildlife Service) in a sea otter in southeastern Alaska. This had previously been found farther north across the Gulf of Alaska, and may prove to be responsible for rapid sea otter declines in western Alaska. Further research has indicated an increasing threat to sea otters (as well as sympatric populations of marine mammals) in the form of phocine distemper virus.

One of the great joys of marine research with wild animals is at the same time a source of great humility. On any given day out in the field, one can witness an event for the first time which literally blows a pet theory right out of the water. Such was the case with transients and sea otters.

On July 9, 2010 I got a call on the radio that there was a small group of killer whales just north of Drake Island. I had been seeing rafts of sea otters in the vicinity and as soon as I got with the five whales (all females and young), they began making lunges past several otters. The otters would surface, snorting and wheezing, some looking roughed-up and injured, pairs holding on to each other and looking around. Some seemed to just disappear, eaten or escaped? A loud shrill repeated call attracted my attention and I watched as a young whale dove underneath a single otter and seemed to be biting its back before leaving it alive. When I approached, it was unable to dive, and appeared to have a broken spine.

The whales became increasingly excited, spyhopping, breaching, lying belly-up and slapping their tail flukes and pectoral fins on the sea surface. They all seemed to converge on another lone otter, one lobtailed on it, one surfaced with the otter in its mouth. After a final whale breach on top of it, several gulls and two bald eagles began circling and I knew the whales were consuming it and leaving scraps of meat or fat at the surface. I retrieved the hydrophone, went in and collected my share for later positive DNA (genetic) identification.

As I had been listening to the sounds the whales were making, my field notes described the most variation I had ever heard in transient calls: *whistles, rooster calls, clicks, rips, taps, honks, farts, burps, low and high chuckles, crunching, rattles, moans, upsliding, sputters, waa, aww, downsliding ohs, screams, grunts, chirps, slaps, motor-growl, repeated scraping sounds, siren calls, many high whistles.*

What it all meant, I can't say for certain. It will be analyzed by those whose field of study is killer whale acoustics. I do know that it wasn't all about food since the whales didn't eat every otter they harassed or mortally injured. It was partly about training the young about a potential food source, however nutritionally deficient. And it doesn't negate the significance of bacterial and viral diseases the otters spread among themselves, which may still be their biggest threats along with environmental degradation. Time will tell us more about whether or not this is a new trend in future feeding habits as other marine mammal species decline.

A memorable encounter

Sometimes even the most peaceful encounters, meaning easy or uneventful, can be revealing and especially memorable. After getting a sighting from one of the tourboats already up Glacier Bay on August 29, 2004, I ran north up the Bay. By the time I got to Drake Island in mid-Bay where it yawns out into a huge "Y," cold winds and big swells were barreling out of the dark wet grayness of the West (left) Arm. I was just talking myself into giving up on the day when I got a sighting on the radio from the Park dispatcher that a kayaker with a hand-held radio had just seen a small group of killer whales at the mouth of Adams Inlet in the East (right) Arm, heading north.

Suddenly, it was worth crashing sideways across the West Arm swell to get to the entrance of the East Arm. As soon as I got there, it was as if I had died and gone to nirvana: Looking northeast all was calm, sunny, no other motor boats, just a few kayaks and four transients for me to follow for the afternoon.

It turned out to be Ranger Jitterbug John in the kayak, but I didn't approach or spoil his wilderness experience. The whales turned out to be male T 87 Harbeson, with his male buddy T 97 Gull, and closer to shore female T 88 Spokane was foraging with female T 90 Eagle. It was obvious T 90's first calf T 90A Eaglet born in 2000 was still not around, and is now considered to be dead. Several of the transient first-born calves have disappeared at a very early age like that, too young to have inclination or training to take off on their own. The females concentrate environmental toxins in their fat-rich breast milk, and pass the highest load of those toxins to the first-born calf. T 90 has since had a second calf T 90B Piglet in 2006, and hopefully having lower toxin loads from its mother's milk will allow it to be healthier in the long run.

As I followed the four transients north through the blissful tranquility of the East Arm that August afternoon in 2004, even the whales seemed to move in slow motion. They began milling slowly just north of Sealers Island, then went rapidly north again. More indecipherable milling close to shore, then all north again. By now we were past the entrance to McBride Glacier, approaching the face of Riggs Glacier and I had certainly followed them farther north in the East Arm than I had followed any whales. They were still very slowly going up Muir Inlet toward Muir Glacier at the end. They seemed ready for a nap, all bunched up together, barely making headway.

We had crossed over the line from White Thunder Ridge over to the Riggs Glacier outwash beach. I always remember that as the course of a one-mile swim Lynne Cox, internationally accomplished cold-water swimmer, swam here in Glacier Bay in early October, 1985. I had assisted Lynne's swim by rowing a tiny dinghy ahead of her to break up the layer of pan ice that had formed on the water surface the night before.

So having communed with the powerful stamina of Lynne Cox, who went on to even more amazing, record-breaking swims, having followed my transient friends to a record-breaking point north in the East Arm, and having a long run home, I left them to their nap. Having been to the face of the Muir Glacier many times myself, I knew they had a chance of running into harbor seal or harbor porpoise in those murky, sediment-rich waters.

During the run back down the smooth turquoise glass of Muir Inlet, I thought about the time quite a few years previous when I had followed some transients into the ice-filled entrance of Johns Hopkins Inlet far up the West Arm. It was getting late in the day, even for summer and all the other boats and ships had long ago headed south toward the entrance of Glacier Bay and on their way out. Although Johns Hopkins Inlet was now open by regulation, the seal pups were weaned and supposedly moving out on their way as well, but for me it was closed by ice. Definitely past time to turn around and get out without denting or breaking that fragile propeller.

The whales were still going farther into the icebergs so I just stopped, took a deep breath and turned off the engine. I looked up and felt instantly engulfed and minimized to a speck in that vast amphitheater of cascading ice. It was that roaring kind of silence from the grinding and popping of the floating ice, from the waterfalls streaming down cliff faces, from fading whale breaths, from the blood in my head. It was the kind of silence and aloneness that makes one savor that delicious terror of being an infinitesimal part of something incomprehensible and beautiful.

Killer whales are just one complex piece of a very complex puzzle of the many Alaskan ecosystems. These pages relate my encounters taken directly from encounter forms I fill out the day they happen. It is not the entire picture or all the answers. I hardly consider myself to be an expert, but these have been my contributions to the efforts to understand how killer whales fit into the larger scheme of life here. They are always irresistible, often unpredictable, bringing an essence of elusive beauty and awe-inspiring wildness into our world. Their place on the planet is theirs alone and could not be filled by anything else as wondrous or enigmatic.

EPILOGUE

May, 2007 / Gustavus, Alaska

The dogs and I have apparently survived the record 215 inches winter snowfall here in southeastern Alaska. For me in Gustavus that meant cross-country skiing on about three to four feet of snow almost every day from November to April. Really good snow, too, not that usual wet coastal slush. I used writing as a way to focus my attention away from the fact that my daughter Eve was spending that same time traveling through Guatemala (where she went to Spanish language school), Nicaragua, Costa Rica, Chile, Argentina, Bolivia and Peru. Through her vivid e-mails, I traveled vicariously.

When I took off in February, 1985 for a month in the Galapagos and Peru, my worried parents had nothing like e-mail to rely on for keeping in touch with me. The day before I returned to the United States from my South American adventures, my parents received a postcard with a Galapagos penguin on the front from me:

Hi, many wild and good times so far. Took me two days to get to Quito, Ecuador due to plane mix-ups... via Guadalahara, Mexico City, Yucatan, Miami, Panama and Colombia. I'm now on a large wooden sailboat in the Galapagos with a bunch of crazy Canadian photographers. Yesterday I saw my first penguins and swam with them. Everything is tame... it's amazing how close one can get. You would love it; start saving your pennies! I'm thinking about going to Machu Picchu in Peru, maybe for the last week. Hope all is well with everyone. Love, Dena

Before Eve left the United States for her Central and South American trip she wrote a letter about her upcoming college graduation and life dreams:

Greetings everyone from vibrant lush Oregon,
Believe it or not, I am graduating June 17, 2006 from the University of Oregon with a Psychology degree (and a lot of art classes under my belt). This is all thoroughly blowing my mind as the last few days of my college experience slip away. The past four years have flown by

faster than I could have ever imagined, as I was wisely told they would. I feel so lucky to have had the opportunity to meet such beautiful people and be a part of such a mind expanding learning environment. I have officially learned how to absorb knowledge and apply it to my external surroundings. I have to say that this is only the beginning of my academic career for I have discovered so many more passions that I desperately want to explore further. Psychology has been the most ideal jumping off point because no matter where I am and what I am doing I will most likely be surrounded by people. It has been fascinating how through becoming more aware and analytical of myself I have come to understand others with more richness and compassion.

I am sure everyone is pondering upon the question of, what will that crazy girl do next? I have many ideas for the future and the list gets longer as each day goes by. A couple of my long term goals are becoming an art therapist or a teacher, but no matter what I do I want to be surrounded by kids and creativity. However, at the present I am going to have to satiate my spirit's more immediate needs as a world traveler, linguist, potter, surfer, mountain climber, sailor, cowgirl, backpacker, gardener, and any fun adventurous hobbies that must be endeavored upon while my mind and body are young. As I am sure many of you know, Elli and I are going to begin with a voyage to Central and South America that should last about a year. We both feel passionately about becoming fluent in Spanish and immersing ourselves in the vibrant Latin culture. I look forward to spending this time together, so we can get to know each other in a new and exciting way.

Currently, I am spending many hours in the ceramic studio learning how to throw pots, build and fire a wood-fire kiln, and simply becoming comfortable in the world of clay. This has been one of the most intense and exciting artistic endeavors for me yet. It is definitely one of my callings, and I hope to dedicate a certain portion of my life to it. Hopefully someday I can share this with you all. I want to thank everyone for your love and support throughout my life. Each one of you has had an impact on me leading up to this day. As for now I want to welcome you all to celebrate this exciting day with me here in Eugene, Oregon or where ever you may be.

Sending you all my love,
Eve Steller Matkin (Age 22)

Eve managed to survive her Central and South American adventures as well (whew!). To stay connected to her at least in spirit, I e-mailed little poems I had created for her that I also translated into Spanish. Since she had invited me to travel with her in that part of the world in the future, I wanted to impress her with how literate and bilingual I was becoming:

Hey runaway bunny
Where are you now?
I miss you so much,
I must find you somehow,
To run through the rushes,
Laugh at the rain,
Gasp at the stars,
Feel a little insane…

Hola conejo desbocado,
Donde estas ahora?
Te extrano en falta bien mucho,
Debo hallar te de algun modo,
Para carrer por las hierbas,
Risa a la lluvia,
Mira a las estrellas,
Siente una pequena insensate…

Eve just returned to Alaska from her seven-country trip, traveling with various friends and family and even alone sometimes. Hard to believe, that shy little girl from Gustavus. In her early teen years, Eve wrote an essay that shares what it was like for her when I worked as a naturalist for the Park and independently studied killer whales. Thanks to the Steller sea lion, in 2001 I was funded again and able to devote future summer seasons mostly to my research, garden and child.

"Alone" by Eve Matkin (Age 14)
I have never liked being alone, it's always been a deep fear of mine. The feeling of knowing that there's nobody there to help you if something happened. When I was younger I used to start crying when my mom didn't come home on time, which always made her feel really guilty. Now I have my dog Orca and he always makes me feel better. I hardly ever feel alone or scared when he's around.

I don't mind being by myself very much anymore. I actually like it because there aren't any distractions while I'm doing my homework and I can call my friends without my mom listening to every word I say. As you get older the fears you had when you were younger start to seem silly. For example, when I was little I used to be scared of monsters and little gremlins. Now just the thought of it seems silly. I am still a little bit afraid of being alone sometimes, at night when I think I hear a noise or after I've watched a freaky movie.

I am nervous about living alone when I get older. While I'm in college I will probably live in a dorm with a roommate. After I get out of school, living alone probably won't be such a big deal but right now that's a long time away and nothing I should be worrying about too much just yet.

When I get scared or feel alone one thing I do is turn on the radio, TV or music so the house seems more full and not so lonely. I am usually very constructive when I'm home alone because I try to keep myself busy. Instead of sitting around being bored I read, cook, paint, do chores, take walks with my dog and just do little things that I haven't had time to do or wanted to do.

Being alone is very important in everybody's life. It's something that everyone needs to do. If I'm frustrated or mad I need to be left alone so I can think things out and cool off. There are times that I need to be with someone, too. When I'm sad, depressed or disappointed I like to talk about it with someone and not keep it bottled up inside.

Being alone does not have to be a bad thing but I don't think it's good to be alone all the time. When I'm alone it's one of the only times I feel like I can act like myself. When you're around other people you're often acting like you think people would want you to act. Another reason being alone is good is that you have time to learn about yourself.

About ten years later, my favorite e-mail from her South American trip was when she was traveling alone in Chile. Here is part of it:

"Solita" (woman alone/on one's own) *by Eve Matkin (Age 23)*
So much has happened since my last update, as there are always so many amazing things flying by when you travel. After some time in busy touristy towns I decided I needed to find something a little more low-key. I decided to head deep into the Andes to this miniscule town. As usual I just hopped on a bus with no plan, but my spirit open to all the possibilities. I stayed on the bus until it stopped and the bus driver decided that I

needed some help. He told me about this place where I could camp on this Mapuche woman's land. He, however, failed to mention that it was about two kilometers out of town. I started walking and finally decided to ask this guy if I was going in the right direction. He was very sweet, as most people are in Chile, and he walked his bike so he could lead me to the place. It was this tiny road with a sign that said Fogon Mapuche and of course said nothing about camping.

  I swear I have a guardian angel with me sometimes. I trudged up to the door of this beautiful structure. Half of it was a wood octagon while the other half was almost entirely made of straw. The bamboo door screeched open and before me stood a weathered old woman dressed in the traditional Mapuche garb. Fixed upon her breast was a silver broach that symbolized the union of family and had been passed down for hundreds of years. She warmly, but looking slightly confused, welcomed me into her home. It was like stepping into a time and a world that I could only imagine in my dreams. There were dried peppers, corn and various herbs hanging from the ceiling. Along the walls there hung sheep skins and hand woven tapestries. There was an ancient spinning wheel tucked away in a corner with yarn spewing forth from it.

  There were wooden tables that looked as if they were growing from the bare earthen floor. The benches all were laden with sheep skin and atop them sat the happiest orange kitten. There was a large fire circle as the center piece that had a cauldron hanging above it from a chain. A funny, thoroughly charred tea pot sat off to the side nestled in the ashes. I couldn't have manifested anything more perfect for my peaceful week of yoga, meditation, Spanish practice and hiking through the beautiful countryside. We sit and chat for a while drinking mate and gazing at the fire. She just couldn't believe that I was alone and had just ever so randomly ended up at her doorstep. It seemed to really befuddle most people that I was a girl traveling alone. I feel that Chile is the safest, most laid back place I have been to, so it didn't seem odd to me.

  I spent most of my days sitting by the stream I was camped next to doing yoga, meditating, reading and writing in my journal. I would take a daily trek off into the mountains stumbling upon spectacular views of volcanoes, crystalline streams and cascading waterfalls. One day I managed to find my own private waterfall tucked away in the woods. I sneaked down from the road making sure that no one saw me. Quickly I stripped off my clothes and jumped in. I was shocked at the bone-breaking frozen waters and leaped out faster than I fell in. I sat there laughing at myself curled up in a ball on a rock. I think a part of me still thought I *was in the tropics where all the water is fairly warm and you can frolic about never getting cold. This water was fresh melt-off from the nearby mountain. It was a perfect hide-away and I savored the tranquil magic of this little place of power.*

Today is Mothers' Day and I am a very happy mother. The cottonwood buds are bursting, the clean fragrance of their fresh oils filling the air with life-affirming sweetness. Hermit thrushes sing their peaceful flute-like song, soothing as the summer rain. They seem to broadcast their melodies more on overcast days, and at the time the sunset glows most colorfully before fading. I am looking forward to planting the garden and spending another season in *Kingfisher*.

What will the killer whales teach me this year? Will my favorite transients show up in Icy Strait and Glacier Bay after their winter of wanderings, some with a new calf to name? I think about the late afternoon I watched T 85 Eve and her third calf T 85C Jasmine as they floated without moving on the glassy surface of Sitakaday Narrows. As the new calf of the year began diving under its mom for short periods of time, I began to smile as I realized T 85 was relaxed enough around me to allow her calf to nurse.

Will we be able to keep the oceans clean enough for the transients to survive at their place at the top of the food chain? How will high mercury levels in sharks affect the future of the offshores? Will interbreeding with oil-spilled Prince William Sound resident pods make our AF and AG pods less healthy over time? Can residents continue to effectively compete with humans' intensive fisheries for salmon and halibut? Can the genetic diversity of all the killer whale cultures world-wide continue to flourish?

Will the hermit thrushes keep coming back every spring? When I stop worrying about all of them and think back on my happiest days on the water, of course times with daughter Eve come to mind… When she was six years old I was able to show her a couple of humpback whales repeatedly bubble-netting out in Icy Strait. The next day she explained bubble-netting to her First Grade class for Show and Tell. Or showing her a porpoise being killed, skinned and shared by transient killer whales. Learning life's lessons together in a beautiful place was always a source of joy.

More recently, there was an encounter with Zorro last summer when my black Labrador retriever Orca (white spot still on his chest) was out at the mouth of Glacier Bay with me. It ended with a rare moment of tranquility with Zorro, Orca and me. Now that he is twelve years old, Orca is about my mom's age in dog years. I can trust him to be a lot more calm in the boat when we are with whales, but he still puts his front paws up on the side of the boat, like a tourist standing at a ship's railing, to see the whales.

About a dozen transients, the large male Zorro included, had just come out of the Bay. They were spread out, milling in sub-groups and making long dives. Not that easy for photo-identification, but I tried my best, then figured the whales may be yakking to each other about what's next. Through the hydrophone the sounds that I described in my field notes: *buzzing, high whistles, whines, up-sliding and down-sliding calls, awww, horn, howl, waa-ooo.* The rest of my notes were about their behavior: *T 63 Zorro joins group with T 86A cow Eider and her new calf T 86A2 Ithuteng. Tail slaps, playing juveniles, spyhops. Zorro very close and slow at boat's stern. Zorro close, circles boat.*

We were just south of Point Gustavus at this point, Orca and I were sitting side-by-side on the back deck of *Kingfisher* drifting with engine off and quiet. I sat with my arms around Orca and whispered in his ear to *Be a good dog*. I said, *Stay*, as Zorro surfaced and exhaled in slow motion, then, "Orca meet Zorro," as we looked up at his jagged dorsal fin towering on the other side of the outboard engines. Through the water, Zorro would have seen a calmly ecstatic researcher and a calmly alert dog.

With his curiosity about the boat, the dog and woman creatures apparently satisfied, the whole transient group took off heading east down Icy Strait. My field notes for that encounter end with *breach, milling, tail slaps, leaping, milling, breach…*

Although it may seem to the average reader that I have had one peak research experience after another, it is truly amazing how much time it really took for them to accumulate. After compiling my computerized database through 2011 and adding up my total effort of time, I found that I had done 1,239 killer whale surveys by boat. This amounted to a total of 492 encounters (some contributed by others) and 5,579 hours of combined searching for or being in the presence of killer whales. Mostly searching and hoping, but apparently enough finding, laughing and learning to keep me moving forward.

Postscript
January, 2008 / Gustavus, Alaska

This morning I woke up to see a clean white world outside. After last night's blizzard, just the top half of the garden fence posts are visible along with a little of the dark green of the spruce branches that aren't buried by the snow. Long clear icicles hang in a connected row from the eaves of the roof, sparkling in the returning sunshine. Some of the snow and ice crystals backed by sun become a prism and shatter the light into a delightful rainbow of colors. The days are getting longer now, I constantly remind myself. Looking out through the icicles, I wonder if Eve's future will be framed in ice. Someday it might not ever look like this again. At the moment she is in Hawaii learning more about earth-sustainable living and organic agriculture.

Stepping outside to be surrounded by so much cold, white, calm and quiet, I am immediately reminded of why I am here. January in Alaska is one of its most special times. Time of the fewest people. Time when the needs of one's life are stripped to the bare essentials: warmth, water, food, friends, books, music, skiing. Hoping that the time for environmental destruction is in the past. The short twilight days in November and December can give one the feeling of swimming through mud, searching for meaning and motivation. The lengthening days of late winter and spring seem to provide both meaning and motivation. I am then reminded it is all so beyond just my efforts and imagined powers to care for my little speck of existence here.

When Eve came back to Gustavus to visit me last summer, we picked berries, ate from the garden, took the dogs for a swim in the Good River and went out for a calm day in the *Kingfisher*. The last time she had been on the water with me we had found T 85 Eve and her offspring making a hidden underwater kill and heard them chatting about it through the hydrophone. This time Eve and I just drifted, sunbathed and chatted.

On her Central and South American travels, she had become fascinated with the art of *poi* or spinning fire. It is basically dancing alone while twirling wire-bound clumps of towel that are at the end of a small chain held in each hand. Two small leather straps attach each chain to two fingers on each hand. The two wrapped towels are covered with gasoline and lit, for a very stunning effect as she whirls the two fireballs gracefully around her. She practiced a lot in the daytime without the fire, then performed with them both lit up the last night of her visit in Gustavus. Of course I was in complete awe and after she left I was compelled to write:

Butterfly of Light

*She comes through my life
like a tornado, spinning fire
from her graceful fingertips,
fire-slashed scars on those
tender wrists.*

*Cool arcing fire
dancing light feet
shimmering eye flashes,
only ashes and footprints
left on the street.*

Post Postscript
February, 2009 / Gustavus, Alaska

It is looking as if we are heading into another year of record-breaking weather. After enduring last summer, which turned out to be the coldest and wettest on record for southeastern Alaska, now it is snowing more than any maniacal cross-country skier could ever wish for. When temperatures sink below zero, the kitchen drain freezes shut. I find myself hoping that the glacier forming around the stovepipe on the roof doesn't tear the stovepipe off when that glacier calves and avalanches down. Icicles attached to the snow hanging from the eaves of the roof curve inward toward the double-paned windows. They look like daggers or frozen fingers beckoning and daring me to come outside.

Standing on the front porch, I notice a large raven up in a nearby spruce tree, munching down snow from the branches around it. I wonder where in all this whiteness is it going to find something more substantial to eat? I remember all the times I have seen them acting so happy-go-lucky as they tuck their wings to perform sideways cartwheels high in the air.

I hear the sweet warbling chirps of the lovely red and brown pine grosbeaks as they move through the high-bush cranberries in the yard. They only eat the large seeds in the remaining berries and leave the skins to stain the snow in bright red spots. I never pick those berries for myself in the fall, knowing the birds will need them more than I do.

Closing my eyes, I try to remember what it is like to stand here in April when the sandhill cranes pass closely overhead by the thousands. They head northwest to land temporarily and feed on the Crane Flats just beyond the Good River, on an ancient migratory pathway that began in California and ends at a nest site in the Arctic. I understand that irresistible pull; it defined my life as well. Their call is a simultaneous growling-chortling-cheeping surge, an overlapping cacophony that fills the air and the mind until there is practically no room for anything else. No negative thoughts, no superficial wanting.

Combined with that warm-moist earth smell that the melting April snow reveals, and the deliciously rich perfume of bursting cottonwood buds, it all registers in my sun-starved brain as pure hope. It is the same feeling I get when I stand here and listen to the yips, howls and croons of a family of wolves out on the Flats nearby. Just knowing they are there being their wild selves is a gift that registers on my face as a slow smile.

Opening my eyes, I see a cow moose, wet and bedraggled, struggling through the deep snow with her calf. They nibble on the bare scraggly twigs of the willow bushes. I feel nothing but compassion for them, and suddenly my life seems a lot easier. Since the last summer moose invasion into the garden, I have begun reinforcing the garden fence, hoping we can coexist here without friction.

As I look out into the garden, the flowery mound of Orca's grave has become smooth and flat from all the snow. On the last day of his life, Orca took off alone for an all-day jaunt. He returned home after dark, soaking wet from an apparently great swim somewhere, and died in his sleep that night. We should all be so lucky! I still have my sweet Remi Rose to keep me company.

After spending last summer in Alaska working at wilderness and art therapy with special needs children and growing big Homer turnips of her own, Eve is again in Hawaii learning more about sustainable agriculture. Lucky girl… although she loves hiking, climbing, skiing, rafting and camping, she has no need to prove how Alaskan she is. I long to go outside and harvest something from the garden right now.

Last summer I encountered offshore killer whales for the second time in about 20 years. It was another large group of about 30 individuals. They were all scattered out in the rain and thick fog west of the entrance to Glacier Bay. Thanks to a sighting from another boater, I managed to find them late in the afternoon heading west toward Cross Sound and the huge Gulf of Alaska.

One of the females (O 96 Sitikit) was traveling separately from the others, and her dorsal fin was chopped completely off just a few inches up from its base. As I looked at her through the view-finder of my camera, trying to photo-identify her for science, my eyes began to fill with tears. I clicked away through the fogging mist as I choked, *What happened to you? That must have hurt so much! I'm so sorry...* As had happened to me many times before, I couldn't witness this with a cold, scientific eye.

It looked as if a huge propeller had sliced it flat off. I left her alone so I could look for the other groups before they disappeared into the darkness, rain and fog closing in around the Inian Islands. If it really was from a boat propeller, was it carelessness or maliciousness that caused it? I thought about the other dangers they faced, that of merely eating.

One of the problems with their liking to eat sharks is that they are constantly and unknowingly exposing themselves to high doses of environmental contaminants such as mercury and other toxic substances. Over the years, long-lived fish such as sharks gradually accumulate these toxins in their tissues, and pass them on up the food chain to the offshore killer whales. The offshores then carry those huge toxin loads in their bodies and mothers pass them on to their offspring through their milk.

Before turning back to home, I wondered if I would ever see them again before they disappeared completely from the ocean. I wondered if our destruction of so much of the natural beauty on this earth is just mindless carelessness or is it our overt selfish maliciousness. Do we have the power and desire to turn things around?

Was my sister's untimely death caused directly or indirectly by toxins in her local environment? So often I find myself wishing I'd had the power to turn the tragic events at the end of her life around. I want to bring her back up here to Alaska to connect her more deeply to my life, to the wonder of these whales' lives. I want to give her the healing balm of learning about the natural world, to transform her spirit, to thank her.

At that moment of watching the offshores fading from sight, it was my deepest hope to turn those whales around from disappearing into the mists of time as so many species before them have gone. I wanted them to turn around, surround my boat so I could reach out to them and say, *Thank you for making this world a more stunning place, thank you for the lessons, thank you for the joy.*

January, 2012
Homer, Alaska

Dear Mama,

    There were still so many things I wanted to tell you and ask you before you died, and still so many things I wanted to do to make you proud of me. I called you the day after your birthday to let you know how well my orca program went that day, but you must have been asleep already, so I sang *Happy Birthday* to your message machine. It seemed appropriate that you were born, married and died all in the month of January. And the night that Kirk made the final decision to let you go, it also seemed appropriate that I was having Homer turnips, beets and salmon for dinner.

    January here in Homer this year has been winter at its most wonderful. Tons of fresh snow on everything gives the delightful illusion of total cleanliness and purity to this earth you loved so dearly. Remi, now about your age in dog years, loves eating snow and ice by the gulping mouthfuls. I can hardly believe how rejuvenated she has become in the cold as she sniffs down the bunny trails. I guess dogs as well as people have the need for a change of scene and new adventures. You would really chuckle at the sight of the resident moose curled up under the window in the morning, covered with a fresh blanket of snow.

    The morning you became all spirit, Remi and I were walking along the quiet snowy road when a huge immature bald eagle swooped low over our heads from behind us. Sweet blessing. I wonder if your perky childlike spirit has already been reincarnated into Eve's new little goat, Daffodil Doris, your being a Capricorn the goat and all. She is super cute and may be birthing some baby goatlets here in a few months. It has been so fun having the opportunity to ski with Eve in such ideal conditions, although she always leaves me in her snow-dust, then waits most sweetly for me to catch up. I wish you could see Eve and Eivin as I left them the other evening, both peacefully knitting glovelets by the fire.

    I'm so happy you got to see the pictures of their wedding last summer. You must have smiled to see the one of Craig and me escorting Eve across the meadow to her future. The ceremony was under an old birch tree overlooking the huge mountains and glaciers beyond the waters of Kachemak Bay. It was one of those times that everyone present seemed to believe in the power of love for the earth and one another. Craig and I sang *Four Strong Winds* together at the reception, my life's theme song for loss and forgiveness in this wounded world.

Last winter while they were traveling together in Thailand, Cambodia and Bali I wrote Eve and Eivin a Valentine poem that reflected some of their adventures they had e-mailed me:

Full moon at my back
first star on my face
wishing like crazy
that you return safe.

It is ok to wander
to cuddle with tigers
so rare and so lovely
they don't seem like fighters.

It is important to see
the effects of our wars
on innocent children
hurt by the scores.

You must witness the temples
that reach to the sky
and feel the great spirits
and souls that can fly.

You may love to dangle
from cliffs by the sea
to proclaim your toughness
above all to feel free.

I see you two swimming
in oceans so blue
oh runaway bunny
my love is still true!

This spring Eve is going to let me be her slave working in her greenhouse and garden to help get things started for her business, Steller Gardens. She wrote up a flyer for her members describing what it is all about and I want to share it with you:

Hello my fellow organic veggie lovers. This is my third year of selling locally grown organic vegetables within this progressive community of Homer. I was born and raised in Alaska and have helped my parents in their gardens since I could walk. I furthered my education after high school at the University of Oregon where I received a bachelor's degree in Psychology. After college I traveled the world and began to take an interest in sustainable agriculture. I took a permaculture design course on the Big Island of Hawaii. This inspired me to jump into gardening and agriculture on a much larger scale. Thus I started a CSA and for those of you who haven't heard of this term before, I will explain it more clearly.

CSA, or Community Supported Agriculture, is a partnership between a local farm and a community of "shareholder" consumers. The shareholders pay an agreed-upon price at the beginning of the summer and receive a weekly supply of vegetables throughout the growing season. In an era when food travels an average of 1500 miles before reaching the dinner plate (and about 3500 miles for Alaskans), the CSA relationship provides a direct link between the production and consumption of locally grown food. As a shareholder, you receive wonderfully fresh and nutritious hand-crafted, high-quality seasonal produce that is picked the day you get it and is grown lovingly without chemical fertilizers, herbicides or pesticides. I practice sustainable ecologically responsible agriculture with a focus on improving soil quality and biodiversity, minimizing fossil fuel input, and working with our natural environment instead of fighting against it. By becoming a member of a CSA you are both receiving beautiful vegetables, and you are also making a difference in how and where your community's food is grown.

Some of our vegetables: beets, carrots, arugula, pak choy, purple mizuna, broccoli, Brussel sprouts, cabbage, romanesque broccoli, cauliflower, celeriac, fennel, edible flowers, stir-fry greens, herbs (chives, marjoram, oregano, parsley, mint, sage, thyme, basil, garlic), kale, kohlrabi, leeks, assorted varieties of lettuce, mesclun mix, onions, parsnips, sugar snap peas, snow peas, hot peppers, potatoes, radishes, shallots, spinach, Swiss and rainbow chard and turnips. There may be an even greater variety this year due to our new high tunnel greenhouse!

Even though I have loved working at the museum here this winter, I must get back to my precious *Kingfisher* and my black and white friends in Glacier Bay come summer. I want to know if T 2 is still hanging out with T 86A Eider and her family. After they joined up last summer, they were inseparable for the rest of the season. I have a distinct impression that he is the father of the yearling, T 86A3 Tyndall, who traveled right next to him, bursting through the water surface with every elated breath.

These are the kind of times that I will feel the ache of wanting to share the moment with you and have you be there. It is some comfort that the essence of your vision and the strong steadfastness of your values seem to have been cloned into Eve. Not to forget a dash of wildness and independence: your favorite childhood story of yourself seemed to be about how you sat backwards on the handlebars of your bicycle and pedaled it forward. Eve did the same thing with horses!

I wish I could show you my recent drawings or call you up to tell you about the latest amazing books I'm reading. I want you to still have the chance to read the ones you missed seeing. Like this one, all finished. It was good you did read it all (except this final letter), but you never got to hold it as a real live book as we both had dreamed.

Thank you for being such a wellspring of inspiration as well as criticism. Who else is there now on this green and blue earth to remind me not to dry my hands on my pants?

As long as I am alive I will remember one of my favorite Christmases. It was the last one you and I spent together at your place in California, a warm and sunny day. No decorations, no elaborate food planning, gifts or bustling hoopla. We were just two aging minimalists sitting side-by-side in the backyard near that irrepressible persimmon tree and the eternally abundant rainbow chard, quietly soaking in a moment of peace.

Love, Dena

SOUTHEASTERN ALASKA KILLER WHALES

RESIDENTS

AF POD

AF 1   Split top (died)
AF 2   Georg (died)
AF 3   Wilhelm (died)
AF 4   Inian
AF 5   Chatham
AF 6   Ancon
AF 7   Hannah (died)
AF 8   Steller
AF 9   Adolphus (died)
AF 10 Dundas
AF 11 Gambier
AF 12 Lazaria
AF 13 Couverden
AF 14 Jonny T
AF 15 Link
AF 16 Muz
AF 17 Coho
AF 18 Frederick
AF 19 Sergius
AF 20 Secret
AF 21 Strawberry
AF 22 Echo II (died)
AF 23 Squaretop
AF 24 Sumner
AF 25 Laguna
AF 26 Tidal
AF 27 Halfmoon
AF 28 Nunatak
AF 29 Pelican
AF 30 Seclusion
AF 31 Althorp
AF 32 Seymour (died)
AF 33 Storm
AF 34 Granite
AF 35 Ruhamah
AF 36 Russell (died)
AF 37 Tenakee
AF 38 Pybus (died)
AF 39 Sol (died)
AF 40 Elfin
AF 41 Cenotaph
AF 42 Nipper
AF 43 Ommaney (died)
AF 44 Shelter
AF 45 Hoonah
AF 46 Chilkat
AF 47 Lituya
AF 48 Sib (died)
AF 49 Endicott
AF 50 Taku
AF 51 Iola
AF 52 Stickeen
AF 53 Tyee (died)
AF 54 Alsek (died)
AF 55 Windfall (died)
AF 56 Warrior
AF 57 Darcy/Wavelet
AF 58 Shaawat (woman)
AF 59 Comber
AF 60 Keetshagoon (offspring or ancestor)
AF 61 Snippet
AF 62 Whitecap
AF 63 Drip
AF 64 Novaya (died?)
AF 65 Esquibel
AF 66 Orcalicious
AF 67 Nevsky
AF 68 Frodo (died?)

AF 69	Latissimus	AG 4	Ripple II
AF 70	Gyatso	AG 5	Lavinia
AF 71	Favorite (died)	AG 6	Lamplugh
AF 72	Lina	AG 7	Nerka (died)
AF 73	Ragtag	AG 8	Newmoon
AF 74	Symphony	AG 9	Graves (died)
AF 75	Zara	AG 10	Misty II
AF 76	Luca	AG 11	Lemesurier
AF 77	Rienga	AG 12	Torch (died)
AF 78	Oakura	AG 13	Hanus
AF 79	Orion	AG 14	Salisbury
AF 80	Elovoi	AG 15	Beartrack
AF 81	Bieli	AG 16	Shag (died)
AF 82	Diki Tsering (Ocean of luck)	AG 17	Zimovia
		AG 18	Cookiecutter
AF 83	Peligrosa	AG 19	Behm
AF 84	Sanuk (playfulness in all things)	AG 20	Spasski
		AG 21	Pete
AF 85	Sunny	AG 22	Samsing
AF 86	Remi	AG 23	Peril
AF 87	Avaaz (voice or song)	AG 24	Marbles
AF 88	Ojos	AG 25	Berg
AF 89	Nebulosa	AG 26	Pinta
AF 90	Wangari	AG 27	Yakobi
AF 91	Maathai	AG 28	Sitakaday
AF 92	Shadow	AG 29	Graffiti
AF 93	Sweepers	AG 30	Situk
AF 94	Blustery	AG 31	Yakutat
AF 95	Thuy	AG 32	Halibut
AF 96	Abuelita	AG 33	Matt
AF 97	Daffodil	AG 34	Straley
AF 98	Abu	AG 35	Helga
AF 99	Cove	AG 36	Clara
AF 100	Iyoukeen	AG 37	Eugenia
AF 101	Amala	AG 38	Wrangelia
		AG 39	Spirit

AG POD

		AG 40	Chirp
AG 1	Oscar (died)	AG 41	Click
AG 2	Carolus (died)	AG 42	Chuckle
AG 3	Gustavus	AG 43	Stosh

AG 44 Capacious
AG 45 Numinous
AG 46 Deeyashk (scarce food)
AG 47 Momo (grandmother)
AG 48 Phoebe II
AG 49 Taylor
AG 50 Koolbeck
AG 51 Kika
AG 52 Ahimsa
AG 53 Hokmah
AG 54 Beyul
AG 55 Sundew

R POD
R 1 Holkham
R 3 Malmsbury
R 4 Noon
R 5 Gardner
R 6 Bananas
R 7 Dall
R 9 Angoon
R 12 Felix
R 13 Bucareli
R 18 Gisborne
R 22 Malleson
R 24 Moran
R 25 Towers
R 26 Porpoise
R 28 Kasiana
R 29 Neva
R 30 Katya
R 31 Cedarleaf
R 34 Lynn
R 38 Gastineau
R 39 Wade
R 47 Refugia
R 50 Kriya

WEST COAST TRANSIENTS

T 1 Charlie Chin (died)
T 2 Florencia (died)
T 2A Yasha (died)
T 2B Pedder
T 2B1 Ricker (died)
T 2C Tasu
T 2C1 Rocky
T 2C2 Barabbas
T 2C3 Helena
T 18 Esperanza
T 19 Mooya
T 19A Pat (died)
T 19B Kosatka (killer whale)
T 19C Spouter
T 23 Warmsprings
T 23C Freshwater
T 23C1 Haat (tides) (died)
T 23C2 Bertha (died)
T 23C3 Durban
T 23D Brighty
T 23D1 Vispera (died)
T 23D2 (died)
T 23D3 Robin
T 24 Gooshdeiheen (water turbulence behind dorsal fin) (died)
T 25 Edgecumbe (died)
T 28 Khaz
T 28A Slocum
T 28B Lydonia
T 28C Lluvia
T 28D Gwaii
T 29 Seaforth (died)
T 31 Drake
T 34 Grace
T 34A Pachamama
T 35 Ruby roo

T 35A	Lester	T 50A	Bolder
T 35A1	Opal	T 50B	Sita
T 36	Flapjack	T 50C	Passage
T 36A	Leland	T 51	Loner
T 36A1	Tierna	T 53	Willoughby (died)
T 36A2	Kailas	T 61	Jim d (died?)
T 36B	Tattertip	T 63	Zorro
T 36B1	Bhotia (teacher)	T 64	Keku
T 36C	Norbulingka (Jewel Park) (died)	T 64A	Minke
		T 64A1	Mawenzi (died)
T 37	Rocky III	T 64A2	Tonsai
T 37A	Volker	T 64B	Amabilidad (kindness)
T 37A1	Inyo (dwelling place of the great spirit)	T 64C	(died)
		T 65	Whidbey II
T 37A2	Inky	T 65A	Fingers
T 37B	Harald	T 65A1	Barco (died)
T 37B1	Lance	T 65A2	Ooxjaa (windy)
T 37C	Visser (died)	T 65A3	Amira (female leader)
T 38	Graeme	T 65A4	Ellifrit
T 38A	Dana	T 65B	Chunk
T 38B	Jane	T 65B1	Birdsall
T 38C	Borrowman	T 66	Muir (died)
T 38D	Falconer	T 68	Yakataga
T 40	T 2	T 68A	Ken
T 41	Lawrie	T 68B	Phylly
T 41A	Jemison	T 68B1	Obsidian
T 41A1	Palm	T 68B2	Quartz
T 44	Whiterock (died)	T 68B3	Wilder
T 48	Roamer (died)	T 68C	Bazan
T 49	Charlotte II (died)	T 68C1	Sila (spirit who rules the weather)
T 49A	Nan		
T 49A1	Noah	T 68C2	(died)
T 49A2	Judy	T 68C3	Jacobsen
T 49A3	Nat	T 68D	Suckling (died)
T 49B	Van	T 71	Bonkers
T 49B1	Voyageur	T 71A	Hopkins
T 49B2	Skyler	T 71B	Hood
T 49C	Janet	T 71C	Jared
T 50	Boulder	T 71D	Heise

T 72	Young	T 89	Buck (died)
T 73	Doris	T 90	Eagle
T 73A	Greg	T 90A	Eaglet (died)
T 73A1	Paws	T 90B	Piglet
T 73A2	Trites	T 90C	Tigger
T 73B	Blur	T 91	Sebree
T 73C	Vicky	T 92	Reid (died)
T 73C1	Guba (powerful storm)	T 93	Joanna
T 73D	Steve	T 94	Idaho (died)
T 74	Andy	T 95	Chichagof (died)
T 75	Kidney	T 96	Strait (big dish) (died)
T 75A	Stone	T 97	Gull
T 75B	Pebbles	T 98	Peratrovich (died)
T 75B1	Scars	T 99	Bella
T 75C	Bam-bam	T 99A	Kirk
T 77	Asja	T 99B	Holly
T 77A	Eva	T 99C	Barakat (spiritual wonderfulness)
T 77B	The Chuch		
T 77C	Neftali	T 100	Hutchins
T 77D	Alcyon (god of calm water)	T 100A	Lucille (died)
		T 100B	Hugh
T 78	Malacca (died)	T 100B1	Freya
T 78A	Gabe (died)	T 100C	Laurel
T 79	Gypsy II (died)	T 100D	Emily (died)
T 82	Huscroft (died)	T 100E	Tharaya (she who illuminates the world)
T 83	Wilf (died)		
T 84	Herb (died)	T 101	Reef
T 85	Eve	T 101A	Rush
T 85A	Zoe	T 101B	Lagoon
T 85B	Alison	T 101C	Lee (died)
T 85C	Jasmine	T 102	Beardslee
T 86	Spider (died)	T 103	Stephens
T 86A	Eider	T 104	Bruce (died)
T 86A1	Nahanni	T 105	Tantallon (take heed of time) (died)
T 86A2	Ithuteng (never stop learning) (died)		
		T 109	Noyes
T 86A3	Tyndall	T 109A	Frio
T 87	Harbeson	T 109A1	(died)
T 88	Spokane (died)	T 109A2	Fuser

T 109A3	Spong	T 150	Mardy
T 109A4	Garrett	T 151	Capricho
T 109B	Sem (psyche)	T 151A	Batalla
T 109B1	(died)	T 151B	Pelagia
T 109B2	(died)	T 162	Sitka
T 109C	Boca	T 163	Augusta (died)
T 109D	Eivin (island wind)	T 165	Thatcher
T 116	Sandy	T 166	Hobart
T 116A	Sturgess	T 166A	Gusty
T 116B	Garforth	T 167	Walpole
T 124	Myrtle	T 168	(died)
T 124A	Kittiwake	T 168A	Bean
T 124A1	Bonapartes	T 168B	(died)
T 124A2	Elkugu	T 169	Chacon
T 124A3	Wasini	T 174	Dixon
T 124A4	Sabio (wise one)	T 174A	Solita
T 124B	Zarembo (died)	T 174B	Jitterbug John
T 124B1	Sean (died)	T 180	Cecil (U 41)
T 124C	Cooper	T 181	Pacific
T 124D	Field	T 181A	Tasman
T 124E	Murk	T 182	Alexandra
T 132	Scott (CA 20)	T 183	Spencer
T 133	Finn (CA 18)	T 183A	Oceania
T 134	Jan (CA 54)	T 184	Biorka
T 135	Dawn (CA 27)	T 188	Dorothy (U 47)
T 137	Loon	T 188A	Craig (U 48)
T 137A	Barb		
T 137B	Tempest		
T 137C	(died)		
T 137D	Wright		

GULF OF ALASKA TRANSIENTS

T 142	Ty
T 143	Ian
T 146	Oamaru
T 146A	Oma
T 146B	Chiloe
T 146C	Svaha! (cry of joy or excitement)
T 146D	Leah
T 146E	Basho

AT 30	Chubby Rain (T 177)
AT 32	Heavy Rain (T 178)
AT 70	Raven's Fire
AT 71	Natoa
AT 72	Goulding
AT 73	Lake
AT 73A	Islas
AT 73B	Otis
AT 74	Kimshan (T 179)

AT 74A Islet (T 179A)
AT 75   Myriad
AT 76   Kukkan
AT 77   Ittar
AT 78   Tawak
AT 79   Borota
AT 80   Klag
AC 13   Bobo
AT 141 Téa
AT 142 Chris
AT 143 Kubwi (big guy)

OFFSHORE KILLER WHALES

AP 1   Barnes
AP 2   Rag
AP 3   Tag
AP 4   Homeshore
AP 5   Excursion (O 144)
AP 6   Groundhog
AP 7   Sisters (O 152)
AP 8   Thorne (O 151)
AP 9   Sweetwater (O 152A)
AP 10 Kai (O 75)
AP 11 Etolin
AP 12 Anjanette
AP 13 Neve
AP 14 Stanhope
O 6   Apa (water)
O 53   Tejo (fire)
O 55   Bain
O 90   Bayu (wind)
O 94   Okasa (sky)
O 96   Sitikit (little bit)
O 282 Slip
O 284 Pritiwi (earth)
O 287 Ginormous

BIBLIOGRAPHY / ALASKAN KILLER WHALE REFERENCES

Barrett-Lennard, L.G., C.O. Matkin, J.W. Durban, E.L. Saulitis and D.K. Ellifrit. 2010. "Predation on gray whales and prolonged feeding on submerged carcasses by transient killer whales at Unimak Island, Alaska." *Marine Ecology Progress Series* 421: 229-241.

Bigg, M.A., G.M. Ellis, J.K.B. Ford and K.C. Balcomb III. 1987. *Killer Whales: A study of their identification, genealogy and natural history in British Columbia and Washington state*. Phantom Press and Publishers, Inc., Nanaimo, British Columbia.

Chadwick, Douglas. 2006. *The Grandest of Lives: Eye to Eye with Whales*. Sierra Club Books, San Francisco, California.

Deecke, V.B., J.K.B. Ford and P.J.B. Slater. 2005. "The vocal behavior of mammal-eating killer whales (*Orcinus orca*): Communicating with costly calls." *Animal Behavior* 69: 395-405.

Deecke, V.B., J.M. Straley, D.R. Matkin and C.M. Gabriele. 2006. "The mammal-eating killer whales of Glacier Bay National Park and Preserve: Hunting with the strong silent types." *Alaska Park Science*. Volume 5, Issue 2. National Park Service, U.S. Department of Interior.

Dolphin, W.F. 1987. "Observations of humpback whale (*Megaptera novaeangliae*) – killer whale (*Orcinus orca*) interactions in Alaska: comparison with terrestrial predator-prey relationships." *Canadian Field Naturalist* 101: 70-75.

Durban, J., D. Ellifrit, M. Dahlheim, J. Waite, C. Matkin, L. Barrett-Lennard, G. Ellis, R. Pitman, R. LeDuc and P. Wade. 2010. "Photographic mark-recapture analysis of clustered mammal-eating killer whales around the Aleutian Islands and Gulf of Alaska." *Marine Biology* 157: 1591-1604.

Ford, Corey. 1966. *Where the Sea Breaks Its Back*. Little, Brown and Company, Canada. Second edition reprinted in 2003 by Alaska Northwest Books.

Ford J.K.B. and G.M. Ellis. 1999. *Transients: Mammal-hunting killer whales*. University of British Columbia Press, Vancouver, British Columbia.

Ford, J.K.B., G.M. Ellis and J.W. Durban. 2008. "An assessment of the potential for recovery of West Coast transient killer whales using coastal waters of British Columbia." Research Document 2007/088 of Fisheries and Oceans Canada.

Ford, J.K.B., G.M. Ellis, D.R. Matkin, K.C. Balcomb, D. Briggs and A.B. Morton. 2005. "Killer whale attacks on minke whales: prey capture and anti-predator tactics." *Marine Mammal Science* 21 (4): 603-618.

Ford, J.K.B., G.M. Ellis, L.G. Barrett-Lennard, A.B. Morton, R.S. Palm and K.C. Balcomb III. 1998. "Dietary specialization in two sympatric populations of killer whales (*Orcinus orca*) in coastal British Columbia and adjacent waters." *Canadian Journal of Zoology* 76: 1456-1471.

Goldstein, T., J. Mazet, V. Gill, A. Doroff, K. Bureck and J. Hammond. 2009. "Phocine distemper virus in northern sea otters in the Pacific Ocean, Alaska, USA." *Emerging Infectious Diseases* 15 (6): 925-927.

Goley, P.D. and J.M. Straley. 1994. "Attack on gray whales (*Eschrichtius robustus*) in Monterey Bay, California, by killer whales (*Orcinus orca*) previously identified in Glacier Bay, Alaska." *Canadian Journal of Zoology* 72: 1528-1530.

Hart, K., V. Gill and K. Kannan. 2008. "Temporal trends (1992-2007) of Perfluorinated chemicals in northern sea otters (*Enhydra lutris kenyoni*) from south-central Alaska." Archives of Environmental Contamination and Toxicology, Springer Science and Business Media, LLC.

Heise, K., L.F. Barrett-Lennard, E. Saulitis, C.O. Matkin and D. Bain. 2003. "Examining the evidence for killer whale predation on Steller sea lions in British Columbia and Alaska." *Aquatic Mammals* 29: 325-334.

Krahn, M., D. Herman, C. Matkin, J. Durban, L. Barrett-Lennard, D. Burrows, M. Dahlheim, N. Black, R. Leduc and P. Wade. 2007. "Use of chemical tracers in assessing the diet and foraging regions of eastern North Pacific killer whales." *Marine Environmental Research* 63 (2): 91-114.

Mathews, E.A. and G.W. Pendleton. 2006. "Declines in harbor seal (*Phoca vitulina*) numbers in Glacier Bay National Park, Alaska, 1992-2002." *Marine Mammal Science* 22 (1): 167-189.

Mathews, E.A. and M.D. Adkison. 2010. "The role of Steller sea lions in a large population decline of harbor seals." *Marine Mammal Science* 26 (4): 803-836.

Matkin, C., J. Durban, E. Saulitis, R. Andrews, J. Straley, D. Matkin and G. Ellis. 2012. "Contrasting abundance and residency patterns of two sympatric populations of transient killer whales in the northern Gulf of Alaska." *Fishery Bulletin* 110: 143-155.

Matkin, C.O., D.R. Matkin, G.M. Ellis, E.L. Saulitis and D. McSweeney. 1997. "Movements of resident killer whales between southeastern Alaska and Prince William Sound, Alaska." *Marine Mammal Science* 13 (3): 469-475.

Matkin, C.O., E.L. Saulitis, G.M. Ellis, P. Olesiuk and S.D. Rice. 2008. "Ongoing population-level impacts on killer whales *Orcinus orca* following the *Exxon Valdez* oil spill in Prince William Sound, Alaska." *Marine Ecology Progress Series* 356: 269-281.

Matkin, C.O., G.M. Ellis, E.L. Saulitis, L.G. Barrett-Lennard and D.R. Matkin. 1999. *Killer Whales of Southern Alaska*. North Gulf Oceanic Society, Homer, Alaska.

Matkin, C.O., L.G. Barrett-Lennard, H. Yurk, D. Ellifrit and A.W. Trites. 2007. "Ecotypic variation and predatory behavior among killer whales (*Orcinus orca*) off the eastern Aleutian Islands, Alaska." *Fishery Bulletin* 105: 74-87.

Matkin, D.R. 2011. "Transient killer whale predation trends in southeastern Alaska." Final Report, Grant #404609, submitted to the U.S. Marine Mammal Commission.

Matkin, D.R., J.M. Straley and C.M. Gabriele. 2007. "Killer whale feeding ecology and non-predatory interactions with other marine mammals in the Glacier Bay region of Alaska." In Piatt, J.F. and S.M. Gende, editors, Proceedings of the Fourth Glacier Bay Science Symposium, 2004. U.S. Geological Survey, Scientific Investigations Report 2007-5047. Pp.155-158.

Norris, Ken. 2010. *Mountain Time: Reflections on the world and our place in it*. University of California Natural Reserve System.

Pitman, R.L., V.B. Deecke, C.M. Gabriele, M. Srinivasan, J.W. Durban, N. Black, E. Mathews, D.R. Matkin, J.L. Neilson, A. Shulman-Janiger, D. Shearwater, P. Stap, J.M. Straley, R. Ternullo and J. Denkinger. 2013. "Too Big to Fail? A review of humpback whale interactions with killer whales." *Mammal Review* (in press).

Saulitis, E., C. Matkin, L. Barrett-Lennard, K. Heise and G. Ellis. 2000. "Foraging strategies of sympatric killer whale (*Orcinus orca*) populations in Prince William Sound, Alaska." *Marine Mammal Science* 16 (1): 94-109.

Saulitis, E.L., C.O. Matkin and F.H. Fay. 2005. "Vocal repertoire and acoustic behavior of the isolated AT1 killer whale sub-population in Southern Alaska." *Canadian Journal of Zoology* 83: 1015-1029.

Saulitis, E.L. 2008. *Leaving Resurrection: Chronicles of a whale scientist*. Boreal Books/ Red Hen Press, Los Angeles, California.

Saulitis, E.L. 2013. *Into Great Silence*. Beacon Press. Boston, Massachusetts.

Towers, J.R., G.M. Ellis and J.K.B. Ford. 2012. "Photo-identification catalogue of Bigg's (transient) killer whales from coastal waters of British Columbia, northern Washington and southeastern Alaska." Canadian Data Report of Fisheries and Aquatic Sciences 1241: v + 127 p.

Wade, P.R., V.N. Burkanov, M.E. Dahlheim, N.A. Friday, L.W. Fritz, T.R. Loughlin, S.A. Mizroch, M.M. Muto, D.W. Rice, L.F. Barrett-Lennard, N.A. Black, A.M. Burdin, J. Calambokidis, S. Cerchio, J.K.B. Ford, J.K. Jacobsen, C.O. Matkin, D.R. Matkin, A.V. Mehta, R.F. Small, J.M. Straley, S.M. McCluskey, G.R. Van Blaricom and P.J. Clapham. 2007. "Killer whales and marine mammal trends in the North Pacific – a re-examination of evidence for sequential magafauna collapse and the prey-switching hypothesis." *Marine Mammal Science* 23: 766-802.

Whalewatcher: "Killer Whale: The Top, Top Predator." Spring 2011. Robert Pitman, editor. *Journal of the American Cetacean Society* 40 (1).

Williams, Terry Tempest. 1991. *Refuge: An Unnatural History of Family and Place*. Pantheon Books/Random House.

Womble, J.N., G.W. Pendleton, E.A. Mathews, G.M. Blundell, N.M. Bool and S.M. Gende. 2010. "Harbor seal (*Phoca vitulina richardii*) decline continues in the rapidly changing landscape of Glacier Bay National Park, Alaska 1992-2008." *Marine Mammal Science* 26 (3): 686-697.

Dena Matkin moved to Homer, Alaska, in 1974 after graduating from the University of California with a degree in Science. She has since worked as a commercial fisherman, naturalist, research biologist, artist and mother. She is a founding member of the North Gulf Oceanic Society and since 1986 she has conducted feeding ecology studies of killer whales in Glacier Bay and Icy Strait, Alaska.

CPSIA information can be obtained at www.ICGtesting.com
Printed in the USA
BVOW10s0146050813

327631BV00003B/4/P